Advance Praise for *Still Christian*

"Evangelicals spend far too much energy 'harmonizing' the Gospels, ensuring that all four evangelists tell the same story. If, however, we want to read the Gospels as permission to tell our own stories of our encounters with Jesus, David Gushee—stripped, of course, of the burdens of canonicity, much less inerrancy—provides a good model. *Still Christian* is an excellent book, both a lover's quarrel and a cautionary tale."

—RANDALL BALMER, John Phillips Professor in Religion, Dartmouth College, and author of *Evangelicalism in America*

"*Still Christian* takes us on the journey of a Christian leader who endeavors to maintain his integrity while navigating his way from a rigid fundamentalism with its right-wing political agenda into a progressive worldview. Gushee describes the conflicts and pains that may have to be endured by any who would dare to make a similar journey. I loved this book!"

—TONY CAMPOLO, Professor Emeritus of Sociology, Eastern University

"David Gushee is one of our finest public theologians in a moment when global life needs public theology reimagined and resurrected. Now he opens his personal journey as a light on this moment of cultural and spiritual reckoning. The story he tells with frankness and vulnerability mirrors that of so many people in this young century—the complexity of being American, Christian, and evangelical and the imperfect and often perilous intersection of theological and biblical conviction with political modes of thinking and operating. Gushee holds all this together with his love of the Gospel and a re_____ __ ___ heart of the Church and of evangelical traditi_____ lic theology had an embodied int_____ thinking on every 'side' of every _____ est questions and confusions alo___ fidelity, David Gushee shows us how this way of being Christian might also be a redemptive force for our time."

—KRISTA TIPPETT, executive producer/host,
On Being; curator, The Civil Conversations Project;
and CEO, Krista Tippett Public Productions

"David Gushee's fascinating memoir will appeal to anyone seeking to understand the complex religious forces shaping American politics and society today. From his conservative Southern Baptist beginnings all the way to his advocacy for LGBT Christians in recent years, Gushee's life and career make for an engrossing account from the front lines of the culture wars. *Still Christian* is essential reading for discovering where the church has come from, where we're headed, and what faithfulness to Jesus looks like when it requires prophetic dissent."

—MATTHEW VINES, executive director, The Reformation
Project, and author of *God and the Gay Christian*

"Testimonies remain an important component of the Christian worship experience, for they reveal how less-than-perfect-humans wrestle with God. *Still Christian* is the testimony of an influential Christian ethicist that embodies what it means to remain faithful. One can learn more about Christian ethics reading Gushee's testimony and then academic theses on the subject."

—MIGUEL A. DE LA TORRE, Professor of Social Ethics and
Latino/a Studies, Iliff School of Theology

"David Gushee is one of the most thoughtful Christian thinkers writing today. *Still Christian* gives an astute and troubling account of the turbulent changes in American evangelical Christianity in recent decades and examines how these changes continue to shape the broader religious landscape. It is also a brave, honest, and deeply personal account of what it means to remain Christian in the early twenty-first century."

—VICTORIA J. BARNETT, general editor,
Dietrich Bonhoeffer Works, English translation series

"David Gushee has written a gripping memoir. His is a life that reveals an amazing journey of faith and startling encounters with the idols that may challenge it. Every chapter brims with the power of his witness: from the moment he gave his life to Jesus, to navigating the inner circles of white American evangelicalism, to finding courage in his faith to speak his truth to power, and now to experiencing sheer joy with his family and grandchild. This is a must-read for anyone trying to walk in faith . . . for anyone trying to live life fully and with purpose."

—EDDIE S. GLAUDE JR., William S. Tod Professor of Religion and African American Studies, and Chair, Center for African American Studies, Princeton University

"David Gushee has written a heartfelt, accessible, deeply personal memoir. *Still Christian* is a moving account of his journey through four decades of asking difficult questions about how Christian faith ought to inform one's positions on the thorniest ethical and political issues of our time. Gushee says he is leaving the white-enculturated and Republican-politicized evangelicalism he has grown up with (and rightly so) but has steadily moved toward the meaning that Jesus gave to the 'evangel' as 'good news' to the poor and the oppressed."

—JIM WALLIS, *New York Times* best-selling author of *America's Original Sin: Racism, White Privilege, and the Bridge to a New America*, president of Sojourners, and editor-in-chief of *Sojourners* magazine

"Writing with a painful honesty, Gushee provides an account of his life with the Baptists that not only helps us understand the struggles that have made him such a humane voice in the so-called evangelical world but also helps those of us outside that world understand it better. Gushee makes clear that *Still Christian* is a testimony not only to mentors like Glen Stassen and Ron Sider but also to the God that refuses to abandon those who call themselves Baptist. Memoirs are fragile genres for theologians, but Gushee's memoir is a must-read for Christians and non-Christians so that both kinds of readers will better understand the challenges of being Christian in this fearful time."

—STANLEY HAUERWAS, Gilbert T. Rowe Professor Emeritus
of Divinity and Law, Duke University Divinity School

"As a thinking person of faith in a world where the church and academy are viewed at odds with one another, David Gushee reveals a vulnerability bound to a firm belief that the lives of those who follow Jesus need to be spent saving souls without losing minds, especially their own. In this compact yet complex autobiography, Gushee unpacks the emotional and ethical baggage of his forty-year journey in a modern-day wilderness with vivid honesty and vital hindsights. Readers will marvel at how he has surveyed as well as survived the ravages of the contemporary culture wars from the front lines armed with his conservative faith, liberal education, and fragile politics. Any scholar wondering why they're still Christian will find solace in his testimony."

—STACEY M. FLOYD-THOMAS, Associate Professor of Ethics
and Society, Vanderbilt University Divinity School

"David Gushee articulates beautifully and personally the journey many Christians today are facing: finding a way to remain 'still Christian' in a complex and challenging world where the black-and-white biblicistic evangelical/fundamentalist faith of one's youth has lost much of its explanatory value. Gushee has lived it, and his courage, conviction, and honesty will certainly resonate with many, as they do with me."

—PETER ENNS, Abram S. Clemens Professor of Biblical
Studies, Eastern University, and author of *The Sin of Certainty*

"It may not seem like it, but American evangelicals are soul searching. Behind closed doors the faith's leaders are asking one critical question, which speaks to the ethical integrity of the evangelical movement itself: How could more born-again Christians vote for an explicitly racist, twice-divorced, nonconservative, non-Christian presidential candidate than for devout, traditional conservatives Bush and Romney? Open, honest, and informed, Christian ethicist David Gushee invites readers of *Still Christian* behind the scenes of the evangelical movement as he interrogates his own evangelical faith roots, journey, and eventual ouster from the movement. *Still Christian* is mandatory reading for such a time as this."

—LISA SHARON HARPER, speaker, activist, and author of
The Very Good Gospel: How Everything Wrong Can Be Made Right

"Bearing witness from intersection of religion, culture, and politics, Gushee tells an insider's tale of the lost battle for the soul of evangelicalism. His writing is by turns searingly honest, elegiac, fascinating, and inspiring. But what does it matter? It matters because many of us, insiders and outsiders to this larger story, know so little about the essentially religious family feud that threatens now to undo our indivisible union. It's time to tune in."

—KEN WILSON, copastor of Blue Ocean Faith, Ann Arbor,
Michigan; author of *A Letter to My Congregation*;
and coauthor with Emily Swan of *Solus Jesus*

"David Gushee is my true brother in all the ways that matter, which is why his new memoir is both beautifully inspiring and heartbreaking to me. Like David, I have spent most of my life hanging onto Jesus in the midst of that relentless storm of anti-intellectual sexism, homophobia, and climate-change denial better known as American evangelicalism, until all I had left was my devotion to loving relationships and social justice and my overwhelming sense of wonder. Unlike me, however, David has come through with both faith and intellect intact, deeply and wisely committed to making the Church more worthy of its founder. As much as I wish he'd come help me pursue goodness in a secular way, this book joyfully testifies to the fact that he's right where he belongs. You Christians are lucky to have him!"

—BART CAMPOLO, humanist chaplain, University of
Southern California, and coauthor with Tony Campolo of
*Why I Left, Why I Stayed: Conversations on Christianity
between an Evangelical Father and His Humanist Son*

"David Gushee has been in almost 'every room where it happens' in American Christianity. From post–Vatican II Catholic, to right-wing evangelical, to radical liberationist, Gushee has been on a surprising spiritual sojourn that offers a singular insight into Christianity in America that is both disturbing and beautiful. *Still Christian* is one part anthropology, one part political history, and one part vocational struggle; yet taken as a whole it is about one man's search for the best way to love Jesus in a complex and conflicted world."

—PAUL BRANDEIS RAUSHENBUSH, senior vice president, Auburn Seminary, and editor of *Voices*

"Like the rings on a tree, David Gushee's life tells a story of the last half century of Christianity in America. We see a Catholic child, a teen convert learning about the Rapture, a curious university student, and a Southern Baptist seminarian (during the Southern Baptist Convention civil war). He was a young man torn between his evangelical faith and his intellectual pursuits, who ended up at one of the most liberal institutions in Christendom. He's been a part of church battles and political battles. He's been the darling of conservatives and progressives. In the end, he is a Christian ethicist who's valiantly followed his conscience. Now that he's quitting the culture wars, we all have a lot to learn from him. These have been tumultuous years for the church in America, and Gushee's autobiography stands as a memorial to all we've gained and lost."

—TONY JONES, author of *Did God Kill Jesus?*

"David Gushee contains multitudes. He's a progressive evangelical Christian who left Catholicism because of weak post–Vatican II catechesis. He seeks justice both for LGBT persons and prenatal children. He's been president of the most important scholarly societies in our field but is also a die-hard political activist and dedicated pastor. Now identifying as 'Batholic,' he has returned to his Catholic faith but without leaving evangelical Christianity. If you suspect that the story of how someone became such an interestingly complex Christ-follower might be worth reading about, you are correct. Christians of all kinds should pick up this readable book—but only if they are ready to be challenged, moved, and inspired."

—CHARLES C. CAMOSY, Associate Professor of
Theological and Social Ethics, Fordham University

"Rev. Dr. David Gushee is one of the most prolific Christian scholars of our time. He has an unusual ability to be extremely proficient in multiple roles: as a professor, an author, a senior leader within his guild, and a pastor. Gushee has had a tremendous shaping effect on the field of Christian ethics, and theological studies, in general. In this book, we have the privilege of seeing into his life behind the scenes. The influence of our shared beloved mentor, the late Glen Stassen, lingers with him and is noticeably present in Gushee's Christian ethics, not as a vocation, but as a way of life."

—REGGIE L. WILLIAMS, Assistant Professor of
Christian Ethics, McCormick Theological Seminary

STILL CHRISTIAN

Also by David P. Gushee
from Westminster John Knox Press

Evangelical Ethics: A Reader

A Letter to My Anxious Christian Friends:
From Fear to Faith in Unsettled Times

STILL CHRISTIAN

Following Jesus Out of
American Evangelicalism

David P. Gushee

WESTMINSTER
JOHN KNOX PRESS
LOUISVILLE · KENTUCKY

© 2017 David P. Gushee

First edition
Published by Westminster John Knox Press
Louisville, Kentucky

17 18 19 20 21 22 23 24 25 26—10 9 8 7 6 5 4 3 2 1

Book design by Erika Lundbom-Krift
Cover design by Mark Abrams
Cover photo by Nick Scheerbart

Library of Congress Cataloging-in-Publication Data

Names: Gushee, David P., 1962- author.
Title: Still Christian : following Jesus out of American evangelicalism / David P. Gushee.
Description: First edition. | Louisville, KY : Westminster John Knox Press, 2017. | Description based on print version record and CIP data provided by publisher; resource not viewed.
Identifiers: LCCN 2017006621 (print) | LCCN 2017029397 (ebook) | ISBN 9781611648270 (ebk.) | ISBN 9780664263379 (pbk. : alk. paper)
Subjects: LCSH: Christianity—United States—20th century. | Christianity—United States—21st century.
Classification: LCC BR526 (ebook) | LCC BR526 .G875 2017 (print) | DDC 277.308/3—dc23
LC record available at https://lccn.loc.gov/2017006621

Most Westminster John Knox Press books are available at special quantity discounts when purchased in bulk by corporations, organizations, and special-interest groups. For more information, please e-mail SpecialSales@wjkbooks.com.

For Jonah, and other grandchildren yet to come

CONTENTS

PREFACE

IT'S NOT LIKE I'M OLD. WELL, I TURNED 55 THIS YEAR, and there's plenty of gray in my beard and more and more in my hair, and my high school yearbook picture is really kind of odd to look at right now. But I've still got some kick left in me, and it's a little early for a deathbed confessional.

I'm not at the end of my journey, I hope. But I am at the end of a major stage of it; that much feels certain. Maybe it's the forty-year thing. As of this writing, I am approaching the forty-year anniversary of the summer of 1978, the season when I set out on the path I've followed ever since. It's when I became what used to be called a born-again Christian.

That year also more or less marks the beginning of a social movement that has constantly intertwined with my own personal journey—and has probably had a lot to do with yours as well. It was the time when fundamentalist and evangelical Christian conservatives were gearing up to create the Christian Right, whose purpose was to take back America for God, primarily by taking effective control of the Republican Party and getting people into power who would advance their agenda. A subplot of that story (in which I would also eventually become entangled) was the fundamentalist takeover of the Southern Baptist Convention.

When I said that simple yes to Jesus in July 1978, I had no earthly idea that my path as a Christian, then a minister, and then an academic, and then an activist, would take me directly into the crosshairs of this movement. I did not know that I would be wrestling in and with Southern Baptist politics, Christian Right politics, evangelical politics, and American politics for forty years. This is an account of what I have experienced in my effort to follow Jesus amid the maelstrom of all this Christian right-wing politics, and a fair amount of Catholic, liberal, mainline, radical, and secular politics as well.

It has been an eventful journey. Somehow right now it feels very much like I am leaving it behind, as if the journey is ending. But I need to try to make sense of it, for me if for nobody else. I need to ask myself how I got here; who I was and who I have now become; and where, if anywhere, was Jesus, the one to whom I have pledged my commitment each day of these forty years. I need to give an account of myself, and make an inquiry into where my God has been in this journey among those battling believers who all claim to be God's people.

And I want to help you understand your own journey up to this point, and the one that lies ahead. At least if we are talking about the American Christian landscape since 1978, I've pretty much seen it all. I was raised a post–Vatican II Catholic, became a Southern Baptist through a mystical teenage conversion, became a Baptist minister, almost abandoned the whole thing for Episcopalianism, discovered liberal-radical Protestantism by full immersion at Union Theological Seminary in New York, almost lost my faith studying the Holocaust, met evangelicals I really liked, met evangelicals I really didn't like, became a Christian ethicist, got a teaching gig at a school that tested my convictions, hung out briefly with really powerful evangelical leaders and helped them figure out some things about abortion and racism, went to a small evangelical college, got involved in national environmental and antitorture activism that embarrassed that university's leaders, moved to a "moderate" university where I was initially distrusted as too conservative, got dazzled and then a bit disillusioned by Barack Obama and his people for a while, became every liberal's favorite evangelical, changed my mind about gay people, wrote a book about it that got me in trouble with a lot of evangelicals, got elected president of the American Academy of Religion and the Society of Christian Ethics, worked against Donald Trump, and taught Sunday School every week to recovering addicts and professors and everyone in between.

When it comes to bitter cultural divisions fueled daily by religion, I'm Forrest Gump. For whatever reason, I've been in the scene, where the conflicts are, where red and blue meet. Like Waldo, if you just look hard enough, you can find me. My journey has taken me through and across and around and amid some of the messiest fights, most interesting moments, and most fascinating people in recent American religious life. I've been on the red side and the blue side, with the Christian Right and the Religious Left, and everyone in between.

If you live in that space as well, if you find that the labels we use to decide whom we can and can't like don't fit you, if you want to look for God outside the boxes the religious wars have tried to put God in, then maybe my journey has something to say about yours.

And here's the thing: I've kept track. Little did these unsuspecting Christians know, but I'm a compulsive journaler and record keeper. I have kept every lecture and speech I've ever given, and pretty much all of my important correspondence. And all along the way, I've been journaling almost every day about most every important thing I've experienced. So I have contemporaneous notes on, for example, the day in 1987 that I was told that white men had better remain quiet in a course on liberation theology, the day in 1995 that I was invited to sell my soul for a nice future working with a conservative seminary president, the evening in 1995 in which the Holy Spirit burned out of me any capacity to hate that same president, the days in 2006 when I received hate mail for opposing torture while my daughter lay unconscious in the hospital, the day in 2007 when I was interrogated intensely for having spent way too long working with conservatives, the day in 2008 when I figured out I was being used by the Obama campaign, and the day in 2011 when a very bright philosopher at a very conservative Christian college said to me, "We know we are supposed to oppose gays, but we can't really give any good reason for it anymore."

Did you notice that I threw a reference to the Holy Spirit into that last paragraph? You see, through all of this, I haven't been able to stop being a Christian. Despite all the fighting, culture warring, and general craziness that I've seen, I am still doing my best to be a follower of Jesus.

And so this journaling, I should tell you, has been prayer journaling. That's mainly how I have prayed for the last forty years—by writing it all out to God. When I became a Christian at the age of 16, it stuck. It took. I can't claim any credit for it, but it's true. And I've been writing it and praying it ever since.

So the stories I am going to tell you are not the stories of a disillusioned ex-Christian. It's weird, perhaps, but none of the nasty stuff I've seen in churches or denominations or seminaries or colleges or academia has ever really had an effect on my faith in Jesus. Jesus isn't the problem. Christians are. So I'm still a Jesus follower after all these years—or trying to be, anyway.

It's not that Christian people are just a problem. People are a mix of good and bad, and the bad is often just a slightly exaggerated version of the good. That's just as true of Christians as it is of everyone else.

We have an expression in the Gushee household, developed by one of our three very clever children when he was a teenager. I like to quote movie lines, and almost every day I do so, whether family members feel like hearing them or not. At one point my son David said of these quotes, "Dad, you never get it exactly right. You never even get it close to right." He said this with a smile, and it has stuck in the family lexicon ever since, along with my mangled quotes from *Ghostbusters, Pee-wee's Big Adventure,* and *Groundhog Day.*

Excuse me for a moment. Back in a second. My wife, Jeanie, called me over to tell me that I am remembering the genesis of "You never get it exactly right" incorrectly. So I guess I never get it exactly right even when it comes to talking about when we started saying that I never get it exactly right.

That Gusheeism is true of Christians, too. We never get it exactly right. We never (or rarely) get it even close to right. But it isn't for lack of trying. Just about everyone I have encountered in the religious landscape of American life over the last forty years has been trying to get it exactly right. And with just a bit of sympathy, one can see how they got to their version of what trying to get it exactly right looks like, even when in the end I, at least, must conclude that they were partly or even largely wrong.

So this is a book that will try to offer a fair rendering of the flawed people and institutions to be found across the red-blue/conservative-liberal barricades in American Christianity. I think it will not be hard to show the virtues of each strand of Christian I have encountered. But it will also be clear how simultaneously these virtues became their own vices. It seems impossible to have any significant amount of a virtue—such as strong conviction—without simultaneously suffering its correlated vice, which is intolerance.

We are experiencing a moment in American life in which our cultural divides have hardened into mutual incomprehension and demonization. I first wrote that line long before the election of Donald Trump as president, and it is even truer now. We don't know each other, we don't understand each other, we don't trust each other, and we don't like each other. All we see are each other's vices, none of each other's virtues. If this memoir from both sides of the barricades helps improve this deplorable situation, that is reason enough to write it.

I may not succeed in this project, because I myself bear a number of scars from the battles in which I have fought. I fear an encroaching bitterness and cynicism in my own soul. The further along I get, the less faith I have in a group called "Christians," and the more I see the world from the perspective of those who have been hurt by Christians. But to give up entirely on Christians or that thing called "the church" would be shattering to me. In lieu of many rounds of expensive therapy to figure all this stuff out, I am doing what I usually do—pondering it all with my pen. Thanks for joining me.

We are where we are because of where we've been. If, like me, you're trying to figure out why Christian life is so fragmented and sometimes destructive today, then it will help to see some of the roads Christians have taken to get here. Because my story has happened along several of those roads, you might find it helpful to hear about it. I think I can open some avenues of understanding related to all kinds of things, such as:

— post–Vatican II U.S. Catholicism compared with Catholicism today
— the Southern Baptist Convention controversy and its warring parties
— mainline liberalism and radicalism

— American conservative and progressive evangelicalism
— life as an academic in both secular and Christian institutions of higher learning
— church life in America in a time of decline
— Christian engagement with politics
— the national media, especially its shrinking band of religion reporters
— culture-war fights over specific issues such as abortion, climate, torture, and LGBT inclusion

So this book will resolve my inner conflicts, profile some fascinating people, dish some really interesting dirt, explain the culture wars—and talk about what God might have to do with any of this.

Jesus grabbed me hard back in 1978, and he has never let me go. Even if my Christian critics think I am beyond redemption, I think Jesus has not yet given up on me. I hope that in these pages his elusive, mysterious, tender, gracious presence will be felt. I hope that becoming a religious professional in a conflicted environment during forty years of culture wars hasn't beaten that tender Jesus out of my soul. Read on and find out.

Chapter 1

GROWING UP,
FINDING JESUS

(1962–1978)

I WAS BORN IN 1962 IN GERMANY. DAD SAYS HE WAS WORK-
ing for the American Chemical Society as an overseas
journalist. I have always wondered whether he was a spy
during the Cold War. (His story is undoubtedly true, but
I prefer mine.)

After I was born, Mom and Dad came back to the
United States and settled in Vienna, Virginia. My sisters
Alice and Janette followed quickly in 1964 and 1965.
Our baby sister, Katey, came along as a surprise in 1970.

Mom and Dad loved each other deeply. Their marriage, especially when we were young, was sometimes
volatile. Both could get riled up. They fought. We saw
it. They made up. We saw it. It was always so good to
see them make up. Their passion for each other was pal-
pable, even if sometimes embarrassing. They married

in 1961, raised us together, retired together, did life together. Many of their friends divorced or were unhappily married. Mom and Dad were neither. I wish every child could have two parents who love each other, and love them, as much as my parents did. I wish every child could have a mom or dad who comforts them when they are sad, brings them little snacks in their room at night just to check in and say hi, and never misses a ballgame. I wish every child could have a dad or mom who, despite being tired at the end of a long day, can be persuaded to get out the catcher's mitt for some fastballs and curveballs in the front yard.

My mother's efforts to raise us as Catholics were desperately unsuccessful. I resigned the faith on the day I was supposed to be committing my life to it. That was the deal I had made with my mother. I would attend the Catholic Church until Confirmation and would only go back on Christmas and Easter after that. This was how it went not only for me but also for my younger sisters.

Mom had no luck getting Dad interested in attending church with us during the 1960s and 1970s, at least not until the very end of their childrearing years. But she soldiered on, dragging us to church each week, sending us to what passed for Christian education classes at that parish, until each of us abandoned ship.

Christian formation in Catholic parishes has historically been handled under a program called Catechumenate in Catholic Doctrine, or CCD. When I was coming through, classes were held in the evenings once a week. Mom made us go to these classes each year, a process culminating in Confirmation.

Unfortunately, in the aftermath of the reforms of

Vatican II (1962–1965), local Catholic formation efforts fell into disarray. I have studied the key documents of Vatican II as an adult, and I believe most of what was accomplished there was profoundly positive. Vatican II reversed the Catholic Church's reflexive resistance to the modern world, opened the church to new ideas, dramatically improved its posture toward the Jewish people, and softened its theological arrogance. The Vatican II documents in social ethics are truly superb, with profound statements on economic justice, colonialism, and peacemaking, among other matters of contemporary concern. I have long considered Vatican II a high point in Catholic history.

But perhaps the progressive openness of Vatican II brought in its wake the theological disorientation of American Catholicism, in that pattern of vice entangled with virtue that is just how the world works. What seemed to trickle down to the Virginia parish of my youth was mainly a loss of confidence in Catholic tradition. The turn toward openness to the onrushing modern world apparently was taken to mean a turn away from ancient Catholic thought and practice. My CCD classes offered little actual instruction in Catholic doctrine. Mom often summarized the content of that program scornfully as "God loves you. Draw a tree." We received no instruction in Augustine or Aquinas, heard nothing about Nicaea or natural law, studied no great saints or martyrs. We got self-actualization and self-esteem and an awful lot of wasted time.

By the time Confirmation came around when I was in eighth grade, there was *nothing there* when it came to a thing called Catholic identity insofar as it related to a kid named David Paul Gushee. The church did attempt to teach a more serious version of Catholic doctrine and tradition at this final Confirmation stage. Priests got involved in our religious education, and they made efforts to walk us through the Nicene Creed. I remember a retreat and an initiation into the tradition of confession. (It was face-to-face with a priest and nowhere to hide—seriously awkward.)

But it was too little, too late. The gap between the great truths of the Catholic tradition and the impious fourteen-year-old kids preparing for Confirmation was insurmountable. I remember looking around at church one day during Confirmation class and thinking, "Not a soul in this group seems to be taking this seriously at all. What a joke!" I left Catholicism at fourteen not because I didn't believe in God or the supernatural, but because I actually thought there might be something supernatural worth believing in—and it apparently wasn't to be found in the Catholic Church.

My post-Confirmation self might be described today as "spiritual but not religious." I was spiritually hungry, though what I mainly remember being hungry for was female attention. This was partly about sex, but my adolescent carnality was softened by my incurable romanticism. I had wanted a special person to call my own since at least second grade, when I fell in love with the little red-haired girl. No joke. From adolescence on, I was frequently inconsolable due to awkward girl-related foul-ups, all dutifully recorded in my notebooks. I let my youngest child read my ninth-grade journal once. She laughed her head off.

Eventually, however, I figured some things out, and

by fall of sophomore year was blessed and afflicted by first love. Let's call her Amanda. She was a pretty brunette, of Southern stock, one year behind me in school. She attended a Southern Baptist congregation with her parents and siblings, though she herself stood in a rebellious posture in relation to the religious expectations there. You see, *at the ripe age of fourteen, Amanda had still not walked the aisle to join the church and get baptized.* She was late, and people were concerned.

Amanda was the first Southern Baptist to cross my path, and so in a very real sense the rest of my story is impossible without her.

Our relationship was a stormy, on-again, off-again affair. We were young. We were clueless about what we were doing, what we were discovering. My journals show me learning a lot, but also flailing around wildly, making many mistakes. I still regret the pain that I brought to Amanda.

In the summer of 1978, I turned sixteen. Back in the day, this meant an immediate trek to get a driver's license and the beginning of breathtaking new freedoms. I was ready for a fresh start of some type; my big baseball career at Oakton High School had already collapsed, my friendships weren't satisfying to me, I didn't like my appearance, and my first love and I were consistently shaky.

One Friday afternoon in mid-July, I was over at Tyson's Corner Mall, checking out the possibility of a gym membership so that I could get fitter and look better at the pool—at that age, life's most important goals. I remember being discouraged by how much it would cost. I walked out of the mall and desultorily looked up the hill. Oddly enough, smack in the middle of this massive mall complex was a little Baptist church. I suddenly remembered that it was the church that Amanda attended, and I had promised her that I would visit it sometime. For some reason, on this particular day, July 14, 1978, I walked up the hill and into the church building. What happened next set the course of my life.

It was a warm, sunny Friday afternoon, so the contrast between the heat of the day and the cool of the church building is the first thing I remember—then the smell of that distinctive cleaning solution scent and the sight of the linoleum floor being waxed to a spit shine. The man at the mop, Bobby Carter, was the first person I met that afternoon. He was a friendly southern type I had not often met by this point in my life, but one I would often meet in the days that followed.

It is not a routine thing in a Baptist church for a strange teenager to wander in on a Friday afternoon looking for something he does not quite know how to name. But Bobby Carter seemed to know just what to do. He took me past the sanctuary and around a little corner to the youth minister, whose name was Kenny Carter and who was laboring in his office on that late Friday afternoon. (The president of the United States at the time was a Southern Baptist named Jimmy Carter. It seemed that most Southern Baptists were named Carter. I made a mental note.) And Kenny Carter, a born evangelist, also knew just what to do. He told me that I had wandered in at a good time. They had a special youth weekend all set up—mini golf that night, on Sunday a great drama group all the way from California, and a Bible study on Monday night. He asked if I might be interested in any of that. I surprised myself by saying yes.

The program that Sunday evening was exotic. A drama group had been invited to take over the evening service and do their thing. They were from California, and they were called the Catalysts. It's amazing that I can still remember that, even before digging out my journal entries from July 1978. I couldn't tell you what their program was about, only what kind of impression it left on me. It communicated the evangelistic Protestant message in a way that I found clear and compelling. Probably all around me were jaded youth who thought it was hokey. But I wasn't one of those jaded youth, and I thought it was profound—profound enough that I decided to return for the Monday night youth Bible study.

The leader this particular night is a memorable figure in my journey. Her name was Chiko Templeman. I honor her in my heart as I remember her. She was a Japanese immigrant. She was a deacon. This is no small detail. Long after 1978, Southern Baptists were still arguing about whether women were biblically qualified to serve as deacons, and this congregation (as I later found out) was hardly cutting-edge liberal. But Chiko Templeman was a deacon, appointed to leadership by the democratic will of a congregation that saw something in her that simply demanded such an appointment. She was also the most mystical, supernaturally wired Baptist person I have ever known. She seemed to have a direct line to God. She would later say that God inspired her to pray for me at specific moments, like 10 a.m. on Tuesday. Every time she told me that, it turns out that there had always been a very good reason for her to have received such an inspiration. That's spine-tingly.

I asked a lot of questions that night. This was a new paradigm for me. Catholics didn't talk about religion the way Chiko did. Your parents get you baptized, take you to church every week, get you to first Communion as a young child. You go to Mass some more, get older, then get confirmed. Then you choose to keep going to church, marry another Catholic, raise your own children in the faith, and then you die. Or something like that.

But Chiko's version of Christianity proposed a definite before and after. You didn't know Jesus, and then you did. Once you did, everything was different. My questions clearly demonstrated that I was one of those who didn't know Jesus. I was discovering this along with others as I listened and asked my questions. I had thought I was a Christian because, after all, I was both baptized and confirmed Catholic. But now . . .

Looking back, I can see a lot of things coming together that night. Kenny Carter was there. That guy was an evangelist. Supernatural-mystical Chiko was there. I am sure that "in her spirit" she knew exactly what was going on with me. And the groovy Catalysts from California were still there. They weren't supposed to be, but the groovy Catalyst van, which bore a striking resemblance to the van in *Scooby-Doo,* wouldn't start that day. So they hung out with us at the Bible study.

I don't know if they drew lots to decide who would follow up with me that night, but the winner was Randy, one of the Catalyst guys. He asked if we could drive around and talk a bit. (That was when people drove around in their cars and talked.) It was late, after 9:30

on a weekday. The Vienna streets were quiet as we drove around in my 1972 Buick Skylark.

I asked questions. He answered. I asked more. He answered more. It got even later. The streets got even quieter. This is how I described it at the time in my journal: *We talked, about God, about Jesus, [Randy] answering my doubting questions and satisfying my intellectual needs. This guy gave me the answers, and he gave me a Jesus and a God who I could finally relate to, talk to. He said, "All your questions are answered now, Dave, and now all you have to do is pray to God and let yourself open up your heart to Jesus and to happiness and to surrender your doubts."*

We ended up back in the parking lot at Providence Baptist. Finally, Randy popped the question: *Randy said, Let God talk to you. Say, "Here God, I'm yours, I give up, please come into my life." And in my own special, different way, I did. Randy and I prayed together, and the words came flowing out of me like never before.*

I opened my eyes and looked at Randy. Something had changed. I go back to my journal for the description: *I felt a welling up inside of me of a tremendous joy, joy like I had never felt, from deep inside. I started trembling and laughing uncontrollably, finally free from doubt and worry, finally accepting God into my life!*

I never saw Randy again. Decades later, I Googled the Catalysts, and they were (of course) nowhere to be found. One thing I did find out shortly after my conversion was that the mysterious van stall apparently occurred because the van had a full gas tank and was parked on a steep hill. As soon as the van was moved to level ground, it started again. I always understood that to be something of a miracle.

No one can offer an indisputable account of the factors that go into a life-changing moment like the one I had with Randy on the evening of July 17, 1978.

For a long time, the only account I had was a straightforwardly supernatural one: God reached out to me when I was low and in need, drawing me up that hill and into that church and over the threshold of salvation four days later. Everything had been supernaturally arranged, just so, from the design of the weekend to the Catalyst van stall to the topic and teacher of the Monday night Bible study. God had a plan for me—unworthy, confused me—and God put that plan into action that weekend, saving my soul and beginning my new life.

Forty years later, I have other accounts available. I could attend to the fragile psychology of a young man of melodramatic emotions, stormy relationships, and unmet spiritual and relational needs, wandering into a church on a Friday afternoon and encountering welcome, vivid faith, and the promise of answers and of peace.

I could ponder the sociology of that congregation at that particular moment in American and Christian history. It includes such factors as the evangelistic emphasis of Southern Baptist churches, the impact of the towering ministry of Billy Graham, the development of a successful formula for converting people to Christianity, the presidency of born-again Baptist Jimmy Carter, and even the residual impact of the Jesus-people movement of the late 1960s and 1970s that produced contemporary forms of gospel presentations like the Catalysts.

I could reduce it to a series of odd coincidences.

There was the striking one that my stormy relationship with Amanda had included a promise to visit her church sometime, as she once visited mine. There was the fact that she was out of town on an agonizing monthlong family vacation, and so our relationship did not distract me that weekend. There was the unplanned presence for one extra day of the Catalysts, whose dramatic sketches on that Sunday night broke through to me. There was the miracle that the most spiritually aware person in the entire church happened to be teaching the Bible study that Monday night. I now know that there is an awful lot of uninspired teaching going on in most churches most days. But this was not one of those days.

Probably everybody has foundational, identity-forming experiences, moments that set the course of their life. This was the most pivotal of mine. Just like Chiko said that night: There was a before. Then there was an after.

All kinds of explanations can be offered about the encounter of sixteen-year-old David Gushee with Jesus-as-mediated-through-these-particular-human-beings that weekend. All kinds of caveats must be expressed about how youthful conversions often fail, about how very much did not change in me and for me, about how many stupid decisions I continued to make for the next several years—and yes, about how the Catholic faith in which I was raised certainly played its own role in forming my spirit and preparing me for a mature Christian life.

But when everything is reviewed, tested, and sifted, I still choose to believe that what I thought happened that night in the old Buick Skylark is what in fact happened: I came into a personal relationship with God through Jesus Christ. I was born again.

If that is not what happened, I literally do not know who I am. That experience so shaped the "I" writing these words that "I" am impossible apart from it.

Chapter 2

A YOUNG CONVERT
FINDS HIS WAY

PROVIDENCE BAPTIST CHURCH
(1978–1980)

As I write this, I've been a Baptist Christian for thirty-nine years. But in the summer of 1978, I was a baby in the faith. I had no idea about this Christian (specifically, Baptist) subculture I was entering. I had no idea how it would compare with other Baptist congregations and institutions I would inhabit over the succeeding decades. All I knew was that I had found Jesus, and I had done it under the auspices of Providence Baptist Church in Tyson's Corner, Virginia, and so I plunged in with pristine naiveté.

And plunge in I did—literally. A month after I prayed with Randy, I was baptized by full immersion at Providence. And for the next two years, I remained immersed in the life of that quirky congregation. It hosted a couple hundred souls in its cozy sanctuary with its wooden pews, smoked glass windows, raised platform for the pastors, choir loft behind, and baptistry for converts like me. The building had plenty of educational space for small groups of all ages, and a fellowship hall for Wednesday night suppers, major events, and an awful lot of drinking of a thing called sweet tea that these transplanted Southerners who found themselves in Northern Virginia really liked. There was also a youth room with groovy Coke-knockoff art painted on the walls with messages like "Jesus—He's the Real Thing," and some couches for sitting around and rapping and stuff.

The pastor was Warren Boling. He was a King James Version preacher—lots of *thees* and *thous* and *thys*. He seemed ancient, though maybe he was younger than I am now. In retrospect, what was perhaps most interesting about him is that his pastorate survived his wife's abandonment of him. By the time I arrived on the scene in the summer of 1978, he was divorced. Every good Southern Baptist knew that the Bible does not allow for divorced pastors. But this congregation allowed its stately old preacher to remain at his post after his wife told him that she just didn't want to be a preacher's wife anymore.

That says something about this particular Northern Virginia Southern Baptist congregation. Somehow, quite early in the timeline of social change, they allowed their personal knowledge of this particular pastor and his tragic situation to triumph over a legalistic reading of the Bible. After all, it does say in 1 Timothy that a pastor is to be the "husband of one wife," and this Southern

Baptist pastor was the husband of zero wives. And Jesus does say in Matthew, "What God has joined together, let no man separate," and this pastor was divorced. But somehow, this church found it possible to decide that Warren Boling was victim, not sinner, and should remain at his post. And so he did.

I like that kind of Christianity better than the alternative. This was an important first encounter with it.

Because we were all in church so much, we sang dozens of hymns, some of them great classics. A number of those old songs planted roots very deep in my soul. They come back to me now, long after the period of my life when I routinely sang them in church. We sang a lot of songs about the blood of Christ and his suffering on the cross:

> Alas! and did my Savior bleed,
> and did my Sovereign die!
> Would he devote that sacred head
> for sinners such as I?

We sang songs about giving everything in your life to Jesus:

> All to Jesus I surrender,
> all to Him I freely give;
> I will ever love and trust Him,
> in His presence daily live.
> I surrender all, I surrender all;
> All to Thee, my blessed Savior,
> I surrender all.

We sang songs about focusing your gaze on Jesus and none other:

Be thou my vision, O Lord of my heart;
naught be all else to me, save that thou art—
thou my best thought, by day or by night;
waking or sleeping, thy presence my light.

We sang songs of gratitude for God's care and provision:

For the beauty of the earth,
for the glory of the skies,
for the love which from our birth
over and around us lies.
Christ, our Lord, to you we raise
this, our hymn of grateful praise.

We sang often of God's redeeming grace:

Amazing grace, how sweet the sound,
that saved a wretch like me!
I once was lost, but now am found,
was blind but now I see.

And we always sang songs of invitation:

Just as I am, without one plea,
but that thy blood was shed for me,
and that thou bidds't me come to thee,
O Lamb of God, I come, I come.

I am quite confident that these are the songs I will remember all the days of my life. They shaped me at least as much as any preaching ever did. They have their limits, but they are in my soul.

They are the songs I sing to my grandson when in his little voice he demands, "Song!"

They are the songs I want people to sing to me when I am making the transition from this life to the next.

Through song and through teaching, Kenny Carter, who was both musician and youth minister, taught me what being a Christian meant. I was a sponge. I soaked up whatever he told me, and did (or tried to do) whatever he told me to do. He was the first major mentor on my journey.

There was plenty of what I would now call "concreteness" in the theology and morality presented to us at Providence Baptist. We were told what we were supposed to believe as Baptists and how we were supposed to live. There was special attention to those particular vices that affect young people.

It was from Kenny and at Providence that I learned clearly that Christians are not supposed to curse. Because I cursed a lot, as my journals attest to an embarrassing degree, this was a major change. Christians are not supposed to have sex outside of marriage, which was always a challenging area for me. Christians are supposed to be on top of their anger and submit it to Christ. I was a very angry young man. Christians are supposed to seek God's will for their major decisions, not just drift into them or go with the crowd; this was also a challenge.

Christians are, it turned out, not supposed to date non-Christians. Therefore, one of the very first things I felt I needed to do as a new Christian was to break up, once and for all, with Amanda. I broke her heart. She wept for days. I don't see how her parents could stand to look at me in the months and years that followed. But they were so very gracious.

It certainly didn't help that over the next two years I dated my way through the Providence youth group. This was absurdly insensitive and deeply wrong. Who

was I, and how could that church have put up with me?
But these church folks had more faith in me than I did in
myself. No matter how raw I was, no matter how many
mistakes I made, the leaders and the people of that congregation responded with love.

When I was elected youth group president and immediately proposed a youth dance party at the church,
rather than shout me down, they appointed a committee
to study the matter. My understanding is that the committee is still hard at work. You see, I didn't know that
Southern Baptists don't dance.

We had one youth program, split into male and
female components, that was supposed to teach us about
the denomination's missionary work. At the end of my
first year at Providence, I took the occasion of the recognition dinner for this program (attended by parents and
other adults) to say that aside from sports, the boys' program did nothing and should be merged with the girls'
program. My fellow congregants grimaced, bit their
tongues, and thanked me for my talk.

They hung in there with me, their mouthy, foolish
convert. In so doing, they taught me a lot about grace,
and church, and second chances, and taking the long
view.

One other thing Kenny taught me that also took hold
was that Christians are supposed to tell everyone about
Jesus. Christians are supposed to feel an urgent sense of
worry over the eternal prospects of everyone they know
and to take every opportunity to tell people about Jesus
before it is too late for them.

The world was divided into two kinds of people:
those who knew Jesus and were going to heaven and

those who did not and were going to hell. Our job was to help move as many from the latter category to the former as we could. This concept became formative in shaping the way I (and many others) looked at the world and lived in it.

I still have the original King James Bible I got from Providence. In the front of that Bible, in pen, are still written about a dozen names of kids at school that I targeted for (always unsuccessful) evangelistic efforts. I remember feeling a deep sense of burden for them. Their names in that old Bible now stand as a permanent memorial to that burden.

Kenny shared this same deep sense of obligation, of course, and on one very memorable occasion, he involved me in a project to win some souls. (I hasten to add that he is not alone in employing the strategy I am about to describe.) We were heading off to a fall youth retreat at Eagle Eyrie, the lovely Baptist camp in the Lynchburg mountains that became the place, five years later, where I proposed to my wife.

Fall retreat. Halloween time. Leaves. Wind. Shadows. It seemed a good time to try to scare the hell out of whatever kids in the Providence contingent had not yet committed their lives to Christ, including Amanda. Kenny (with my help) recorded what can only be called a terroristic tape in which we mixed our voices crying for relief from the fires of hell. "I'm burning. . . . Help me. . . . If only I had accepted Jesus while there was time . . . [cue desperate moaning sounds]." There probably are still some people in counseling due to that weekend.

I am deeply regretful that I had any part of that effort

to manipulate people into a profession of faith. Many have left Christianity because of the doctrine of hell and because of those kinds of pressure tactics. Yet it is interesting to contrast the fervor of Christians who still retain something of that sense of urgency and mission with those who have abandoned it altogether. Vices and virtues intertwined. I prefer evangelical urgency to liberal complacency, but the object of that urgency also matters. Perhaps you have been there.

My full immersion into youth group included participating in some of the fads of the time:

— speculations about the timetable for Jesus' (supposedly imminent) return and the end of the world, and songs about the Rapture, such as "You've Been Left Behind"
— Dallas Baptist pastor W. A. Criswell's book *Why I Preach That the Bible Is Literally True*
— an audiotape series on why speaking in tongues and other "charismatic" practices were of the devil
— arguments that the wine referred to in the New Testament was in fact grape juice, further evidence for Baptist opposition to alcohol consumption

What kind of church was this? What kind of church has women deacons, and a divorced pastor, and Kenny Carter, and Hal Lindsey and W. A. Criswell, and the Rapture, and youth basketball, and "quiet times," and a mystical Japanese woman leading Bible studies? And did I mention the church lady who recruited me for a bit part in a video put out by the Conservative Caucus called "Can Soviet Imperialism Be Stopped?" in which I played a Soviet soldier greedily pouring red Communist paint all over the world? (If anyone has that footage, please send it to me. I'll pay good money, and my students will appreciate it very much.) What kind of church was this? It was a typical Southern Baptist/evangelical congregation, before the great sorting, before the religious wars of the 1980s and 1990s, before it became necessary for congregations and individuals to take sides in the increasingly rancorous and divisive battles that have left us where we are—certain that if those with whom we disagree can't be our kind of Christian, they can't be Christian at all.

Providence Baptist stood at that moment on the brink of the great sundering, on the Southern Baptist front of the American cultural wars. But at that moment, before the beginning of an organized political campaign to take the Southern Baptists firmly and clearly to the right, their life—like that of American Christians across the denominational spectrum—was an often riotous, deeply incoherent diversity held together by some shared songs, publications, and mission efforts. Dramatically different personalities, congregations, theologies, styles, and regions of the country all existed under one denominational tent, and all were accommodated. For so many Christians, that unity in diversity is as gone as the Providence Baptist Church that I knew over at Tyson's Corner in 1978, long ago sold and bulldozed to make room for more shopping.

Within a month of my baptism, the Providence kids foolishly elected me president of their little youth group. Within a year, I "felt called to the ministry." My senior picture in the high school yearbook—hopelessly air-brushed, of course—says that my goal is "to become a Southern Baptist pastor." My journal entry from April 24, 1979, just nine months after my conversion, already has me articulating that vocation: *Serving God is my life-time's calling. . . . I know that if I perform to my potential, God will eventually use me as a minister of His Word.*

I became that.

By the time I graduated from high school at 18, two major pillars of my identity were in place, pillars that have not fallen yet and by God's grace will never fall: I was a committed Christian in a growing personal relationship with Jesus, and I was called to the Christian ministry. I have been attempting to live out those commitments ever since. Still Christian after all these years. But what a journey it has been.

Chapter 3

LOVING THE QUESTIONS BUT NOT ALWAYS THE PEOPLE

COLLEGE AND SEMINARY
(1980–1987)

THE WILLIAM & MARY YEARS

Unlike many born-and-bred Southern Baptists, going to a Baptist college was not an option for me. My college choices consisted of precisely all the state universities in Virginia. I ended up going to the College of William & Mary and never regretted it.

It did not take long for me to decide to major in religion and minor in sociology, which turned out to be nice precursors to the vocation of Christian ethics that I discovered later. Religion at William & Mary was taught pretty much in a pure "religious studies" mode. This meant that all classes were taught in a descriptive vein rather than from any explicit faith perspective. Whatever it was that any of our professors believed, we would never find out.

But the faculty was quite good. I was especially taken by Tom Finn, a former Catholic priest with flowing white hair and cool sweaters who used to stride up and down the lecture aisles teaching us some serious New Testament. I recall vividly his first words on the first day of his popular class on Christian origins. He asked a large lecture hall full of students, "Did Jesus of Nazareth really rise from the dead?" My earnest young Baptist self was aghast. How could anyone ask such a question? It's right there in the New Testament! It's the core belief of my entire faith!

Dr. Finn proceeded to take us through modern critical study of the New Testament, dropping in the kinds of questions along the way that are now commonplace: Did Paul really write the Pastoral Epistles? Did Jesus really perform miracles? Are there layers of editing in the New Testament as there are in the Hebrew Bible? (Editing?) What is the relationship between belief and truth in the arena of religion?

I remember more than a few anxious moments trying to bring together the Southern Baptist literalism/fundamentalism that dominated my formative youth group years with questions such as these. Many of us who teach seminary students find the same thing happens to seminarians if it has not already taken place in college. When Sunday School faith meets scholarship in religion, many crises of faith can ensue. I have spent much of my adult life trying to help young people make the transition from brittle certainties to a more supple and mature faith that usually (but not always) leaves them stronger for having wrestled with the tough questions.

It didn't take long for me to figure out that these struggles, while uncomfortable, were also the source of growth. I was not going to run away from the hard questions raised in my classes, but neither was I going to throw up my hands in despair. I would lean into the questions while attempting to hold onto the beliefs that were most important.

This reflection from the summer after my freshman year in college foreshadows much about my later journey: *Amy Grant sings, "You must put aside the reasoning that's standing in the way." Well, my convictions may be shaky but this one isn't—I will never sacrifice my intellect on the altar of "being faithful." If you [God] can't stand up to my measly questions, then you must be an illusion. . . . Must I sacrifice my intellect for the faith? No, I will not suppress my mind, I will not give up my intellect. I will give up the faith first.*

By senior year, I was moving full speed ahead. The most important development was that I asked Jeanie Grant to marry me in October late on a windy night at Eagle Eyrie Retreat Center outside Lynchburg. She said yes, in one of the most thrilling moments of my life.

A gorgeous petite blonde of devout faith, high character, lively intellect, and artistic sensibility, Jeanie was the answer to my tortured quest for that one special person who would love me and whom I could love.

I know this about myself: If I had married the wrong person, ending up miserable or divorced, I might never have recovered. I know myself to have a certain kind of emotional fragility and deep dependence on happiness in love. On those occasions over three and a half decades when Jeanie and I have struggled, I have barely been functional. Some people seem to be able to compartmentalize personal heartache from work achievement. I believe that I could not have achieved that. I am so grateful to Jeanie, and for her, in ways too numerous to recount.

Soon it became time to figure out what to do next. Despite all that had changed in me, I still wanted to be a Southern Baptist pastor. Around me I had significant academic voices, including that of Tom Finn, saying I had a fine academic career ahead of me if I wanted to choose that route. I decided to pursue master's studies in religion, which would open a path either to ministry or to academia.

But where? Everyone in my Baptist circles said it needed to be either Southeastern Baptist Theological Seminary in North Carolina or the flagship Southern Baptist Theological Seminary in Louisville. Tom Finn begged me to look at schools like Harvard and Yale. He was sure I could get into an elite school and that such a school would launch a great academic career for me. He said that going to a Baptist seminary that anyone could get into would be a real waste of my talents.

This was a fork in the road. Harvard or Southern? Which was it going to be?

I do not recall it being that much of a struggle. I was by now six years into my Baptist convert's journey. I had been thoroughly socialized into the Southern Baptist subculture. I had had largely happy early experiences in Baptist ministry at my local church and in the Baptist Student Union at William & Mary. My soon-to-be bride was a Southern Baptist girl. I still felt called to be a Southern Baptist minister. My most significant role models were all Southern Baptist ministers who had gone to one or another of these Baptist schools. So on August 12, 1984, Jeanie and I packed up our little U-Haul van and drove from Falls Church, Virginia, to Louisville for me to begin seminary and Jeanie to start nursing school. She was 21, I was 22, and we had only been married for eight days. Thus began one further, fateful step into an entanglement with the southern Baptists from which I have never quite escaped.

What would my life (our life, my family's life) have been like if instead of going west to Louisville we had gone north to Harvard? Who would I have become? Who would we have become? I cannot pretend that I do not sometimes wish we had pointed the van north. I sometimes wish fifty-five-year-old me could tell twenty-two-year-old me that Baptist life was going to be a bloody mess, that I would be up to my eyeballs in Baptist conflict, that all my teaching posts would be in Baptist schools, that I would eventually have to leave the Southern Baptists, and that my wife and children would abandon the Baptists altogether.

I seem to have even anticipated that it was going to be a difficult road. I wrote this in my journal on Christmas Eve, 1980: *I've been wondering where God wants me as a minister. For a while I was sure it was the Baptist church. Yet I surely am an atypical Baptist. I haven't ruled out any denomination, though by all indications from God I will be a Baptist. Could be a somewhat stormy association, but it's in God's hands.*

The kid was right. But four years later, Jeanie and

I drove to Louisville, pursuing God's will as we understood it.

THE SOUTHERN SEMINARY YEARS

For those unacquainted with Southern Baptists, it is hard to describe the sheer massiveness of the enterprise of theological education in what is, despite recent declines, still the largest Protestant denomination in America. As I write, I teach in a seminary that will count it a success this fall if the student body reaches 180, served by a full-time faculty of twelve. When I wandered onto the campus of *The* Southern Baptist Theological Seminary in the fall semester of 1984, I joined a community of three thousand students served by a full-time faculty of about seventy. And Southern was just one of six denominational seminaries. Southern Baptists, numbering an estimated fifteen million at the time, produced, trained, and employed a whole heap of ministers. I was getting ready to become one of them.

But change was in the air. The Southern Seminary where I arrived in 1984 was embroiled in a fierce denominational controversy that would shadow me from the opening convocation until, well, now. Little known to me before my arrival was the fact that Southern Baptists were at the forefront of the religious wars of the 1980s and beyond, and that Southern Seminary was ground zero. I showed up in the midst of the carefully organized campaign of "fundamentalist-conservatives" to take over (back?) the denomination from "moderate" (moderate-conservative? liberal?) control. The ambiguity is intentional, because competing explanations of what was going on were and are possible.

From the perspective of those who then held power in the denomination and in the seminary (the so-called moderates), the story was this: The Southern Baptist Convention was under assault by a faction of highly politicized fundamentalists (who preferred to be called conservatives, or sometimes evangelicals). These adversaries were based mainly in Texas and were led by theologian Paige Patterson and judge-activist Paul Pressler. They had figured out that they could gain total control of the denomination and all of its national-level institutions, including the seminaries, if they could simply win the presidential election every year at the annual meeting of the Southern Baptist Convention (SBC). They would need to put forward politically committed candidates of their faction. If victorious, these men would use their two-year terms to appoint only people from their faction to the trustee boards of SBC institutions. If they did this long enough, they could take control of the denomination and its institutions. They would do so in the name of defending the Bible and defeating theological liberalism.

This is exactly the strategy they were in the middle of executing when I arrived on the Southern Seminary campus in 1984. The fundamentalists won their first SBC presidential election in 1979 and by the fall of 1984 had won six straight elections. The fight would be over by 1993, after nine more victories.

The agenda of the SBC moderates was to preserve control of the denomination and the seminary for their side and its way of doing higher education and being Baptist. While they were derided as liberals by the conservatives, I never met a true theological liberal faculty member the whole time I was at Southern Seminary. In biblical studies, most professors did teach a modest version of historical criticism, but it was hardly outré compared to what I ran across later in my educational pilgrimage. I found that my theology professors hardly strayed to the "left" of Karl Barth, and legends like Dale Moody were very, very Southern Baptist. No, those Southern Seminary faculty were still pious Southern Baptist folks who were simply reasonably open to the broader world of ideas and wanted their students exposed to that world. They also, of course, like most academics, feared witch hunts, purges, and attacks on their academic freedom. Already by 1984, the academic environment was becoming more conservative and less free.

Those identifying with the conservative side saw it very differently. They believed that the denomination as a whole, and the seminaries and colleges in particular, were straying into mainline liberalism, including an eroding belief in the truthfulness and authority of the Bible. They feared that the students they were sending to Southern and other schools were going to be corrupted by their education and come back useless. It was common in my experience to hear Southern Baptist conservatives tell stories of being mocked in class by students and even professors for their conservative beliefs. A seething anger at what they experienced as disrespectful liberal elitism became a powerful part of their motivation. (Sound familiar? Such anger at liberal disdain was articulated during and after the 2016 election by Trump voters. Remember the response to Hillary Clinton's comment about the "basket of deplorables"? It is a very powerful force.)

Both sides believed that they were the true Southern Baptists. Both believed they ought to lead the denomination and its institutions. For decades they had shared power despite their differences. But during the conservative resurgence, as the winning side called it, it became a zero-sum game. One side would win, and the other would leave.

With the hindsight of thirty years, it's easy to see how the SBC controversy was deeply connected to—indeed, rooted in—secular politics, the rise of the Christian Right, and what became known as the culture wars.

Those wars had intertwined but distinctive battle-fronts. On the religious side, the Southern Baptist fights were the most visible. But in Brian McLaren's 2016 book, *The Great Spiritual Migration,* he describes a political fundamentalist takeover of the whole of evangelical Christianity, not just the Southern Baptists. I think he is probably right. A movement of once-considerable theological and moral diversity was gradually and intentionally moved to a place of conservative theological and moral rigidity.

On the political front, Republicans had been attempting to shift the South from Democrat to Republican since the 1960s. The Republicans' "Southern strategy" included both direct and veiled appeals to white discomfort with black gains achieved via the civil rights movement. The more that national Democratic leaders such as Lyndon Johnson threw their support to black civil rights and racial integration, the more the South became ripe for a Republican resurgence.

Republicans certainly made gains with white Southerners in this way and continue to do so. But millions of white Southerners are, or want to be, devout and faithful Christians. A struggle was set up for the white Southern Christian soul between the racial reconciliation central to the gospel and the sometimes veiled, sometimes open racism central to white, especially Southern, culture. Of course, this struggle is as old as America itself, having become entrenched where slavery was prevalent. We have seen all too often that in the conflict between gospel reconciliation and racism in Southern—even Southern evangelical—contexts, racism wins.

By the late 1970s, a different strategy was developed on the conservative side, focusing especially on traditionalist Christian discomfort with the women's movement, the sexual revolution, and the 1973 *Roe v. Wade* decision on abortion. The culture wars were born, pitting against each other those favoring and those opposing these liberalizing cultural and legal developments. This proved a more appealing agenda for conservative Christian consumption than directly attacking progress in racial integration and black empowerment.

Prosecuting the culture wars then became the main agenda of the Christian Right, led by white Southern pastors and activists such as Jerry Falwell and Pat Robertson, which adopted a political strategy of aligning with the Republicans to reverse the social changes of the 1960s and 1970s. The Christian Right led especially with abortion but also included issues related to sex, gender, and family life. The Christian Right wanted to gain control of Republican social policy. In return, it would help Republican candidates get elected. It also wanted to gain control of the Southern Baptist Convention.

The year 1979 is exceedingly important in this tale. Just as that was the year the Southern Baptist conservative resurgence won its first presidential victory, it was also the year that the Christian Right was coalescing around Jerry Falwell and his cohort to take out the moderate Southern Baptist president Jimmy Carter, defeat the moderate Republicans, and win the presidency for the hardline conservative Republican candidate Ronald Reagan. Some of the same people working on the secular political front were also waging the Southern Baptist fight.

In 1979, I was seventeen and had been a Christian for less than a year. I had no idea what I was getting into.

Given the atmosphere of religious warfare that I quickly discovered at Southern Seminary in 1984, it's not surprising that very early in my first semester I strongly considered leaving to go to one of those elite divinity schools in the North that Tom Finn had recommended. I was not excited about Southern Baptist culture wars. I did not feel at home with all these born-and-bred Southern Baptists. I found the coursework and classroom environment somewhat constricted compared to what I had been doing at William & Mary, and I wanted to spread my wings a bit more. And Jeanie and I were not particularly enjoying delivering newspapers twice a day to put food on the table.

In October 1984, I produced a stack of ten letters of inquiry to other schools. They were stamped and sitting by the door, ready to be mailed. What would my future, our future, have been if they had gone out? I wrote this in my journal at that time: *I am a member of two communities, both of which are hostile to each other. I am a Southern Baptist, loyal to its deepest traditions and values, and well-nourished by [its] evangelical pietism. . . . Meanwhile, I am an intellectual, very interested in things of the mind . . . very open to the fruits of modern scholarship . . . and very much interested in being a top-flight member of that community. [I have] big dreams: Harvard, Yale, Chicago. . . . The Southern Baptists think the Ivies are pagan, pointy-headed intellectuals, and the Ivies consider the Baptists a backward people . . . with absolutely no grasp of the modern world. . . . Can I straddle both worlds?*

Still torn, I pulled back. We were newly married and had just moved to our first home. I had a shot at a job as a youth minister for a major local congregation, St. Matthews Baptist Church. I had also quickly discovered the field of Christian ethics that first year at Southern and with it a community, a mentor, and a dawning sense of vocation.

So we hung in there to the end, both graduating in the spring of 1987—Jeanie as a nurse, me with a master of divinity—and with our first baby on the way.

One major reason that I stayed at Southern was my new mentor, Glen Stassen. Glen was to become one of my closest friends and most important mentors. The course of my journey is inconceivable apart from his role as a model, teacher, mentor, colleague, and all-around advocate who fiercely pried open doors for me and others all the days of his adult life.

Glen, who died in 2014 and whose loss I still feel very keenly, was wholly committed to not just the discipline of Christian ethics but to the way of Christ, which was for him inextricably connected to the discipline of Christian ethics. It is not nearly enough to say that he was a scholar who researched Christian ethics, or a teacher who taught Christian ethics, or an activist who marched for Christian ethics. Glen lived and breathed Christian ethics, in all of these dimensions, all at the same time, all more or less continuously. He wasn't a person who had a job. He was a person utterly consumed by his vocation.

It affected everything. He drove beat-up old cars, and as infrequently as possible, in order to resist consumerism and to protect the environment. He stayed in the cheapest possible hotels, sharing rooms and skipping meals, to be a good steward and not buy into the high life. He wore the same clothes for as long as they could possibly hold out, and then longer. He cared nothing for material things, hardly bothered to cash his honoraria and royalty checks, and gave back portions of his salary when that could help his school add more ethics teachers.

Glen was driven, to put it mildly. He came from a driven family: His father was Harold Stassen, the youngest governor in Minnesota history, a hero in World War II, one of the founders of the United Nations, head of the Arms Control and Disarmament Agency, and a serious presidential candidate for a while. Glen was a liberal in the Minnesota populist tradition, like his father, though his father was a Republican when it was possible to be both liberal and Republican.

Glen was a voracious reader in anything related to Christian social ethics, and his office was an amazingly disheveled pile of articles, books, student papers, newspapers, lecture notes, apple cores, you name it. I have never managed to read as much as Glen did, but his interests became mine, and many of his mentors became imprinted on my soul. Those interests include the Holocaust and nuclear weapons, and those mentors include Dietrich Bonhoeffer and Martin Luther King Jr. whose works I inhaled under Glen's influence.

It cannot have been easy to be a family member of one so purely and wholly devoted to his craft and to the way of Jesus. But as a mentor, Glen was pretty much ideal. He oozed from every pore that this Christian ethics thing is truly a life worth living, the best discipline ever, and worth your very, very best.

But even though Glen always remained a loyal Baptist, I still wasn't all that happy with the denomination and its controversies, and Jeanie was also very open to a change. In the fall of 1986, finally free of weekly Baptist church ministry responsibilities after leaving St. Matthews, Jeanie and I undertook the course of inquiry required to join the Episcopal Church.

It's easy to see why this might be of interest from my side, given the drama going on in my Southern Baptist world, and I haven't even mentioned how miserable that plum youth ministry job was—miserable enough to make it clear that I must never attempt to be a full-time Baptist minister. But a denominational change was also of interest to lifetime Southern Baptist girl Jeanie Gushee, who had been developing a considerable attraction to the more historic, less parochial, more liturgical, more aesthetically pleasing Roman Catholic Church that I had left behind as a teenager—or, better, never actually discovered. The Episcopal Church could possibly be a place where we could meet in the middle.

And we almost did. But after undertaking the entire three-month inquiry process, we decided not to leave the Southern Baptists. I was ordained at my college Baptist church in April 1987. We were just not quite ready to pull the trigger on both a religious identity and professional career change at the same time, so close to the end of the seminary journey. We stayed with the Baptists yet again.

Still, the desire to spread my wings and explore a new part of the Christian world remained strong. I decided to apply for doctoral programs in Christian ethics that were only in the North and only non-Baptist. Glen played a key role in persuading me that my best choice was to go to the liberal-mainline Union Theological Seminary in New York. I was going to write about nuclear weapons and Christian ethics, and we were going to live on the Upper West Side of Manhattan.

With my pregnant wife, I went to New York in mid-August 1987, anticipating with great excitement the prospect of becoming a doctoral student, and soon, a father. On the eve of the move, I wrote this: *We are on a raft together, about to go over the waterfall, clinging tightly to each other. O God, we need you now more than ever. Please journey with us to Babylon.*

Chapter 4

LOOKING FOR A PLACE AMONG THE LIBERALS

UNION THEOLOGICAL SEMINARY IN NEW YORK (1987–1989)

IF I FELT LIKE A FISH OUT OF WATER AT SOUTHERN BAPTIST Theological Seminary, the experience paled in comparison to what I encountered at Union Theological Seminary in New York. Jeanie and I spent just two years in residence on that Upper Manhattan campus, in part because of that deep sense of not belonging. Yet I now see that Union marked me more deeply than I could possibly have anticipated when we abandoned residence there in the summer of 1989.

Union Seminary has a long and storied history, beginning with its founding in the early nineteenth century as a Presbyterian school. I was most familiar with it through two names: Reinhold Niebuhr and Dietrich Bonhoeffer. Niebuhr was the towering leader of mainline Christian social ethics from the 1930s through the early 1960s. I studied him closely in the summer of 1987 and then in work with my primary advisor, Larry Rasmussen. Bonhoeffer, of course, was the brilliant German scholar who twice came to Union in the 1930s—first for postdoctoral study, then later as a potential refugee from Nazi Germany. I could hardly name two scholars who loomed larger in the development of my own ethical vision than Niebuhr and Bonhoeffer. Niebuhr modeled for me the peripatetic life of scholarly, popular, and church engagement that I have since tried to pursue, and Bonhoeffer's heroic journey from a childhood of great privilege to becoming a martyred anti-Nazi resister—as well as his fascinating theology and ethics—never ceases to inspire me.

From the 1960s into the period that I was there, Union largely transitioned from mainline Protestant liberalism to liberationist Protestant radicalism. It became a headquarters for new contextual theologies: black liberation theology with James Cone, third-world liberation theology, feminist theologies, womanist theologies, and LGBT/queer theologies. The watchword was liberation from oppression, and the center of gravity moved from white male Europeans and Americans such as Bonhoeffer and Niebuhr to previously marginalized voices offering perspectives explicitly tied to their "minoritized" race, gender, ethnicity, nationality, and/or sexuality.

This was the world I entered in the warm summer of 1987. In my limited Christian sojourn to this point, I had never seen anything like it. My Southern Baptist churches, William & Mary's religion department, and Southern Seminary had all been very white, very male, very straight, very Southern, very American institutions.

I was quite unprepared for the experience I was about to have at Union, recommended to me by Glen Stassen without any mention of any of this.

I got a taste of what was to come on the very first day of my very first class. The topic was third-world liberation theology, the professor was the famous James Cone, and white males were a definite minority in the class. On that first day, Dr. Cone offered a scorching condemnation of white, male, Euro-American oppression and at least an implicit "by any means necessary" call for liberation.

With the foolish confidence of an ignorant, entitled white guy, I was the first to raise a question after his lecture: "Dr. Cone, it seems as if you are advocating violence here. Is that appropriate for Christian theology?"—or something like that. I remember his answer better than my question. He launched into a disquisition on how that is always the first question that privileged white males like myself ask when oppressed people begin talking about liberation. As I recall, then he said, "This is a class where it is our questions, not yours, that will be central. For this reason, it will be important for our white male brothers in this class to listen and not to talk during this semester."

We're not in Louisville anymore, Toto. I felt humiliated and silenced, angry and bewildered. I was going to have to learn these new ground rules before I ruined myself in that little community, whose ideological spectrum stretched all the way from "liberals to radicals," as one professor memorably and unironically put it. I was neither, and I was going to have to learn to manage my self-presentation accordingly. In terms of the broader

Union community, I mainly managed by staying quiet. I learned my lesson well, but at the cost of closing myself off from any deep engagement with the people and ideas I was meeting for the first time.

Identity politics is a term that often marches in lockstep with *political correctness* in the vocabulary of white male resentment. I will admit that I was certainly drawn to such concepts at the beginning of my experience at Union. For the first time in my life, people seemed to be defining themselves by their identity and to be sizing me up negatively based solely on my identity: my nationality, my gender, my sexuality, and my marital status. This was new, and I did not like it.

I vividly remember the first day of a seminar class with one of my two primary ethics mentors, Beverly Harrison, a legendary radical Protestant feminist (who was always good to me, I might add). All we had done was look at the syllabus, as I recall, and I had remained silent. No problem, right? But at the break I was standing in the hallway with a white female student. We were chatting; I recall that she was smoking. She said to me quite casually, "I don't like people who look like you." Punched in the gut, I sputtered, "And what is that?" She replied, "You know, white, male, all-American-boy types." What was I supposed to say to that?

It is probably not a surprise that I found this environment uncomfortable and looked for safety elsewhere. That safe place was home, of course. Jeanie was pregnant, and our first little one, Holly, our "New York baby," was born on a very cold night in January 1988. I spent a lot of precious moments with baby Holly, because Jeanie soon went back to work and I had a significant share of daddy duty. I had no real experience with babies, as was evidenced by these words that I wrote three days after Holly was born: *It is very hard work taking care of a baby, especially in those crying times. My heart is in my throat when she cries and cries. I frantically search for what is wrong as my pulse races and my body tenses. But I know that if I keep working at it, soon it will come much easier.*

Another place I could find refuge was at church. Our decision about where to go to church illuminates our state of mind at the time. With the towering Riverside Church literally in our backyard, the amazingly beautiful Cathedral of St. John the Divine just eight blocks away, and Harlem's famous Abyssinian Baptist Church to our north, we instead chose to go to little Metro Baptist Church eighty blocks south.

And at Union itself, I hung out primarily with white Baptists, Lutherans, and other somewhat recognizable types from my prior experience. This is how I described the overall situation after one year of doctoral work: *There is a major social / ideological gulf between me and most people at Union. . . . I am more conservative than people here. I resist their slogans. . . . Politically I am sympathetic with liberation movements but grow weary of the rhetoric . . . praxis, solidarity, disempowerment. . . . I need to be the best of what I am—a politically / theologically moderate scholar . . . [which means being viewed as] conservative at UTS and liberal at SBTS.*

I now see those two years as a missed opportunity in many ways. Overwhelmed by the radicalism of the community and by my own sense of vulnerability there, I participated little in community life. I almost never went to chapel, ate infrequently in the gorgeous refectory, and rarely attended extra lectures or other community events. I could have learned so much about other ways of understanding God, other life experiences, other journeys of faith. I sometimes wish I could go back and find that frightened, aloof young man and tell him to relax a little bit, to open up, to listen and learn. Today, all I can do is forgive him.

Still, my actual degree program experience was successful. I found an excellent mentor in Larry Rasmussen, who held the prestigious Reinhold Niebuhr chair in ethics and who was a fantastic supervisor. Glen Stassen had steered me in the direction of Union in large part because he knew and respected Larry, and because the three of us had a deep shared interest in nuclear weapons and peacemaking. Once on campus, I learned that Larry also had done extensive work on Dietrich Bonhoeffer and was working on a book on Reinhold Niebuhr—for which I became his research assistant. With this amiable, unthreatening, very gifted Lutheran ethicist, I could relax, and I was able to do good work for him both in the classroom and as his assistant. Mentors are everything in life. I have often told Larry how deeply I appreciate him.

When I entered Union, my plan was to write a dissertation on the ethics of nuclear deterrence. The context was the Cold War. Ronald Reagan was in his second term as president, and especially early in his term, the nuclear standoff with the Soviet Union seemed quite terrifying to me. I took classes both at Union and at Columbia University to this end.

But in the fall of 1989, the Berlin Wall fell. By 1991 the Soviet Union had collapsed, simply ceasing to exist.

These astonishing developments led me to the conclusion that there was no reason to write about the nuclear arms race between two countries, one of which no longer existed. If I had had better foresight, I might have thought to ask what was going to happen with all these weapons and whether ethical considerations might still be relevant. But like most people, I mistakenly equated the end of the Cold War with the end of the nuclear weapons problem. That problem remains very much with us today.

Instead my attention turned to the Holocaust—potentially, a theologically dangerous decision. What I mean is that the kinds of people I was reading, especially on the Christian side, were arguing that traditional Christian theology had fed the development of Christian anti-Judaism, which was fundamental to a broader pattern of Christian Jew-hatred that developed over two millennia. This Jew-hatred, often called anti-Semitism, was an indispensable prerequisite to the Holocaust.

In other words, the Holocaust was not just a random explosion of genocidal hatred on the part of one evil twentieth-century regime, but instead reflected a two-thousand-year buildup of contempt for Jews, rooted in Christianity itself. If this was the case, Christian theological response to the Holocaust must try to go to the roots of Christian theological anti-Judaism and remove the elements that have been so disastrous for Jews. Among those elements might lie such core Christian convictions as the messiahship and resurrection of Jesus.

After I presented a not-very-successful conference paper dealing with these questions, my thinking about the Holocaust—and my academic career in general—received a boost. I heard a Jewish sociologist named Lawrence Baron present what I found to be terribly interesting work on devout Christian rescuers of Jews during the Holocaust. He described what he was learning about their actions and their motivations, but then he invited his Christian scholarly listeners to get into this research because we would have a better chance of understanding the theological thinking and language of these rescuers.

At that moment I realized I had my dissertation topic. I would write about what motivated Christians to rescue Jews, and what contemporary Christian ethics could learn from that. I worked on that dissertation from 1990 to 1993 and then published the work with Fortress Press as *The Righteous Gentiles of the Holocaust: A Christian Interpretation* in 1994. It was the launch of my publishing career.

It was also deeply formative for my way of looking at Christian faith and ethics. Some core discoveries and commitments have never left me: Christianity, per se, can produce either bad fruit or good fruit, so Christianity itself is never to be uncritically celebrated. Christian theology had a problem with Jews and Judaism from its very beginning, and it has produced consistently bad fruit. To begin to name this is to puncture forever any kind of happy Christian triumphalism about how wonderful we are.

But the good news is that minority strands of Christianity sometimes contain surprising resources for pro-Jewish theology, and all Christianity has the potential to produce the good fruit of compassion, mercy, and justice if the way of Jesus is properly taught and modeled. Still, during the Holocaust, most Christians were passive bystanders and some were actively lethal to Jews. Only a tiny minority rescued Jews.

To get to rescuing Jews, Christians needed a *theology* that at least did not prevent their rescuing and might even encourage it, an *ethic* that motivated rescuing based on a commitment to honoring life's sacredness and advancing justice, a *heart* capable of compassion toward suffering people, and *courage* to do what their ethic and their emotions motivated them to do. This proved to be the path of a definite minority. So the task of Christian ethics is to produce more of these hardy, resistant, compassionate, courageous, rescuing souls and fewer of everyone else. That gives us plenty to do, and it is always an uphill struggle. This task became my vocation.

Much of the agonizing work involved in writing my dissertation took place in Raleigh, North Carolina, and then in Philadelphia. We moved to Raleigh in the summer of 1989 when Union chose to sell its building at 527 Riverside Drive. We did not like New York that much anyway, and with friends and child care promised in Raleigh, we moved there.

Eighteen months, five comprehensive exams, and one more child later (our dear son, David), we moved to Philadelphia for me to take up a full-time job to support my growing family. I wrote my dissertation mainly at night for the better part of thirty months. With little babies sleeping all around me, I wrote about a place and time where babies were cruelly murdered and occasionally saved. My sleep was haunted by nightmares involving murdered children.

How can I describe the impact of Union Seminary

on my life? In the six years from 1987 to 1993, I earned an M.Phil. and Ph.D. and gained the credentialing necessary for my career. We had three children, apparently setting a record in Union doctoral student history. Seeds were planted in me for a much deeper concern for the voices of the marginalized in both world and church, but my white-guy resistance prevented much growth from those seeds for a long while.

Unexpectedly, a love of New York City was also planted, and this also gradually blossomed. As the years went by, Jeanie and I mainly remembered the cool stuff about the city rather than our earlier fears and frustrations. Most years we find a way to get to New York for a weekend or two.

Meanwhile, Union has claimed me as its alumnus, giving me a Unitas Award a few years ago during a lovely evening that included warm congratulations from James Cone. I am now proud to claim Union as it has claimed me.

Indeed, one way to understand my overall journey is that in the end, Union Seminary became more and more pivotal the further I got from it. But it wasn't just a matter of time. It was only when I began to stand up for a few particularly marginalized groups, and began to experience marginalization for doing so, that the insights and commitments of Union became precious to me. Praxis, solidarity, disempowerment, resistance, liberation, a God of the oppressed—it finally all made sense.

But that is to get ahead of my story.

Chapter 5

FINDING A PLACE AMONG THE EVANGELICAL LEFT

EVANGELICALS FOR SOCIAL ACTION
(1990–1993)

I NEEDED A JOB. WE WERE LIVING IN RALEIGH, NORTH Carolina. Jeanie was working as a nurse at Wake Medical Center. For fifteen months, I had been employed only as a full-time comprehensive-exam-taker and then dissertation-proposaler, living far away from New York while pursuing my work based on the distant hope that I would one day finish at Union. Money was tight.

By the summer of 1990, I had gotten through doctoral exams and was beginning to work on my dissertation prospectus. But with Jeanie now pregnant with our second child, I decided that I could no longer leave it to Jeanie, plus family help, to be the sole source of support for us financially. I began looking for the jobs that might be available to someone with my rather limited credentials: an M.Div. from Southern, and now the in-course M.Phil. from Union.

That opportunity arrived in Philadelphia. My name had been given to Ron Sider, president of Evangelicals for Social Action and professor at Eastern Baptist Theological Seminary. Ron was a radical evangelical Christian. He wanted me for editorial work on his magazine, then called the *ESA Advocate*. Jeanie and I bought a lovely old Victorian house in the gritty Germantown area, and I began a thirty-month run with Ron, another pivotal mentor in my career.

Ron is of Canadian Mennonite stock, and everything about his life reflected (and still does) the deep historical commitments of this Radical Reformation church tradition. Ron was committed to biblical inspiration and authority, finding in the Bible a demand for economic simplicity, concern for the poor, and pacifism. He identified strongly with the broader evangelical tradition and seemed to know pretty much everybody worth knowing in the evangelical world. He was devout in his practice of Christian piety and lived an admirably austere personal lifestyle.

By the time I joined Ron's enterprise in 1990, he was a controversial celebrity in evangelical Christianity. His 1975 book, *Rich Christians in an Age of Hunger*, argued that it was unbiblical for rich first-world Christians to pursue standard consumerism when we live among "a billion hungry neighbors." He laid verse after verse from the Bible against the reality both of North American wealth and Global South misery. He said that we were like the rich man ignoring poor Lazarus at our gates and that collectively and individually we would be judged for this sin against God and the poor.

Ron practiced what he preached. He chose to live in urban Philadelphia rather than the posh suburbs. He drove a very old car. He and his wife adopted a child from Latin America. And he practiced the graduated tithe—that is, the more money he made, the higher the percentage he gave away. Ron was the real deal. He reminded me of Glen Stassen. In fact, the two of them knew and respected each other.

Ron faced scalding criticism for his stance on poverty from within the evangelical world. Much of his career was spent fending off attacks from evangelicals who did not like his book or its implications. (This should have been a warning to me.) Ron once showed me a copy of a book written specifically to mock him: *Productive Christians in an Age of Guilt-Manipulators*. He handed it to me with a sly smile. You know you've done something when people take the time to write entire books opposing you.

Ron Sider was the first person who introduced me in a serious way to this religious community called evangelicals. Southern Baptists were *Southern Baptists* and had never called themselves evangelicals to this point in history (more on that later). Mainline liberals certainly weren't evangelicals.

But Ron was an evangelical. He spoke of this community with great respect, despite the criticism he had received from some within it. It was important to him to be viewed as a legitimate evangelical and to participate in evangelical life both in North America and around the world. Ron understood that he represented one branch of evangelicalism, a radical evangelicalism from the Anabaptist tradition, and he was confident that this voice needed representation. But he considered himself part of the broader evangelical community and related widely with it.

This is as good a time as any for me to offer a sketch of what that elusive word *evangelical* means and where it comes from. The modern use of *evangelical* in the U.S. context traces back to the World War II era. American Protestantism had been split into two primary camps since the late nineteenth and early twentieth centuries. These two camps were sometimes called fundamentalists and modernists, or fundamentalists and liberal/mainline Protestants. They had divided over a number of issues, most notably whether to accept the findings and potential implications of historical-critical study of the Bible, and whether to accept the theory of evolution and its implications for reading the Bible. Fundamentalists said no to these scientific approaches, and mainline Protestants generally said yes.

Mainline Protestants had control of most of the major Protestant theological seminaries (Princeton, Harvard, Yale, Chicago, Union, etc.) and the major Protestant denominations, such as those known today as the Presbyterian Church (U.S.A.), the United Methodist Church, the Evangelical Lutheran Church in America, and the Episcopal Church. They emphasized ecumenical dialogue and cooperative work and formed the Federal (later the National) Council of Churches for these efforts. Fundamentalists, alarmed by what they considered serious theological drift in these denominations and seminaries, and inclined toward hair-splitting doctrinal distinctions, either refused to affiliate with the mainline Protestants or withdrew from existing affiliations at some time during the fundamentalist-modernist controversy.

Evangelicalism was the term retrieved by World War II–era leaders such as Carl F. H. Henry and E. J. Carnell to name a reformed fundamentalism eager to engage the broader world but without abandoning fundamental convictions of Protestant orthodoxy. Theologically, they tried to focus on the essential doctrines without getting tangled up with secondary matters such as exactly when and how Jesus was coming back. But they remained quite conservative in their understanding of the nature and authority of the Bible.

I was taught to see fundamentalism and evangelicalism as distinct communities of conservative Protestants, and they can be looked at in that way. But hard experience over several decades leads me now to conclude that evangelicalism was in one sense a rebranding effort on the part of a cadre of smart fundamentalists around 1945. The rebranding stuck, and so *evangelical* came to mean that type of Protestant Christian who is neither fundamentalist nor liberal/mainline.

Those who wanted to leave fundamentalism behind and be rebranded as evangelicals made energetic efforts to create and sustain this new identity. They did not claim that it was new, but instead traced a lineage all the way back to the Reformation (or to the early church) and to reformist and pietist movements within Protestantism ever since. To claim the term *evangelical* for oneself was to mean "true gospel Christian" or "true Reformation Christian," as opposed to hard-bitten fundamentalist or liberal compromiser.

The new evangelicals of the postwar era built a host of significant new institutions, most of which I later served in my own journey. Fuller Theological Seminary, *Christianity Today* magazine, and the National Association of Evangelicals are three of the most important. In addition, a host of pre–World War II denominations, educational institutions, publishing houses, and parachurch organizations chose voluntarily to rebrand themselves as evangelical or as part of the evangelical movement, often leaving an earlier fundamentalist label behind.

Evangelicalism thus became a sprawling movement of groups that in earlier eras would have had little to do with each other, ranging from doctrinaire Calvinists to tongue-speaking Pentecostals to warm-hearted Pietists to peace-loving Mennonites. And this is not to speak of the half-in, half-out evangelicals of color, such as black, Hispanic, and Asian-American evangelicals who shared much evangelical theology but who had often been segregated into separate denominational bodies and who still have an uneasy relationship to mainstream—that is, white—evangelicalism.

Meanwhile, because evangelicals are almost by definition evangelistic, throughout the late twentieth century, the movement and the label spread globally as well, so that there are a whole host of self-identified evangelical institutions around the world, now dwarfing the prior mainline Protestant presence in many lands.

All of this preceded the rise of the Christian Right in the late 1970s. And even though that particular right-wing movement increasingly came to own the evangelical label in public perception, that was a late development and was met with strong resistance by other evangelicals such as Ron Sider.

So perhaps the world I entered by joining Ron in Philadelphia in 1990 is starting to fill in a bit: Here was a left-leaning Mennonite, a card-carrying evangelical, but an anti-Christian-Right evangelical trying to call other evangelicals to social action of a particular type and avoiding mere pietism, mere evangelism, or merely right-wing politics.

Ron was not the only character on the scene attempting to do this. Nor was his Evangelicals for Social Action the only organization. He enjoyed good, if sometimes competitive, friendships with others of his type in the evangelical community. Men such as Tony Campolo of Eastern College and John Alexander (founder of a now-defunct community and magazine called The Other Side), both also based in Philadelphia, and Jim Wallis (leader of the Sojourners community), based in Washington, D.C., also emerged in the late 1960s and 1970s as representatives of an evangelical left.

Their understanding of evangelical Christianity led to very different moral and political conclusions than people like Jerry Falwell and Pat Robertson adduced from the faith. They were focused on poverty, race, and war. They were gender egalitarians and environmentalists. They cared about and lived in urban America. They voted Democrat. They were not opposed to the sex-and-abortion agenda of the right, but they focused elsewhere. And all of this was rooted in prayerful, church-based, Bible-focused evangelical piety.

I found it enormously appealing. It seemed that my quest for a spiritual and intellectual home had come to its end. I was not a right-wing Southern Baptist or a fan of the Christian Right. I was not a left-wing mainline or radical Protestant. I was a Sider-type evangelical.

Yet while deeply fulfilling in many ways, my time at Evangelicals for Social Action made clear to me that what I wanted was the academic life, full stop. I wrote about this in a journal entry in April 1992: *My vocation is the full-time academic life. I want to be Dr. Gushee, professor of religion / Christian ethics at _____. I want a book-lined office, tweed jackets, syllabi, student meetings, committee meetings, lectures, tests, books, writing, lecturing. On a quiet, leafy campus. . . . This is the life I want, and I want it as soon as possible.*

It is possible that if Eastern Baptist Theological Seminary (out of whose basement Evangelicals for Social Action operated) had a bit more money around 1992, I would have had a permanent career on that modestly leafy campus, possibly combined with work at Evangelicals for Social Action. My first teaching experiences happened at Eastern in 1991, and they were delightful. The seminary's president told me, "The students are ecstatic about your teaching." What a wonderful thing for a rookie professor to hear!

But there were no full-time jobs there at that time. So I sought an academic job in the 1992–1993 year, knowing that I would have that new doctoral degree in May

1993 and hoping against hope that I would be among the minority of newly minted Ph.D.'s who could find a full-time tenure-track post. Finding that first academic job, however, was a humbling process. I applied for every relevant position in Christian ethics, but to no avail. The "meat market" at the annual American Academy of Religion meeting was especially discouraging. But in mid-February 1993, after all those years of grueling work, including writing a dissertation at night and working all day for thirty months, I received a most unexpected phone call from Louisville.

The man on the other end of the line was David Dockery. He was the young dean and incoming provost of . . . Southern Baptist Theological Seminary. Alma mater, hail. The conservative takeover of the Southern Baptist Convention had been nearly completed. Southern Seminary president Roy Honeycutt and provost Larry McSwain were leaving at the end of the spring 1993 term. Ethicist Paul Simmons had just been forced out for showing an explicit film about the sex lives of disabled people, giving his long-time enemies just enough rope with which to hang him.

David Dockery now needed to find a Christian ethicist who could be acceptable (if such a thing were possible) both to the "old" moderate faculty, very much aggrieved and anxious, and to the new trustees, now with a conservative majority, who were about to name a new president. Glen Stassen, still teaching at Southern, recommended me and very much wanted me to come. He thought that I might be a candidate who could thread that very narrow needle. Young, relatively unformed, a self-identified evangelical, pro-life on abortion, committed to justice and peace, a Southern Seminary graduate—I might be just the ticket.

Southern offered me the job, and I said yes.

Recently I discovered a letter that I wrote to friends and family on May 27, 1993. It announced that we were moving to Louisville on June 20 with our three kids: Holly, then five, David, two and a half, and baby Marie, eight months. "God willing, we want to settle down now . . . and build a life together in Louisville," the letter stated. I continued:

> I am walking—eyes open—into an institution in transition. Southern has lost thirty-five faculty members in the last three years. . . . This year it will inaugurate a new president. Two deans and the provost recently have resigned. More staff changes appear to be ahead. The institution needs your prayers, as do I as I join the faculty.

I then gave four reasons why I would take a job at such an institution: "the opportunity to have an impact on thousands of ministers," the discovery that "my vision for Christian ethics and seminary education was largely congruent" with that of the search committee, the chance to perhaps be part of "helping chart a constructive way ahead" for a transitioning Southern Seminary, and finally, the fact that "Southern was willing to give me a job—in a very tough job market."

That latter reason was the main one. I had a Ph.D., and I wanted to teach. Southern Seminary was my only job offer. I had to take it, despite the risks of a transitioning seminary, despite having attended a Presbyterian Church for three years and having no strong desire to return to the Southern Baptists, and despite feeling more at home in the Sider-type progressive evangelical world than anywhere else.

The next three years in Louisville proved to be something like a crucible. Or a trial by fire. Or just wretched.

Chapter 6

FINDING A VOICE WHILE NOT LOSING A SOUL

YOUNG PROFESSOR AT SOUTHERN SEMINARY (1993–1996)

NO PERIOD OF MY LIFE HAS SEEMED MORE OPAQUE TO ME, more elusive to my own self-understanding, than the years of my first full-time teaching assignment, at Southern Baptist Theological Seminary in Louisville. The period was filled with pain—for me personally, for my colleagues, and for the seminary as a whole. But I faced choices during that period that were excruciating and that in later years I had never fully reviewed.

I knew that this was the first stage of my life in which my actions were being taken seriously by others—in which there was a public figure named David Gushee who was making decisions that were affecting others, who had a certain kind of image that was related in some quite imperfect way to *who I really was*, if any such stability of person and character can be said to have existed at that time in my life.

The process of writing this book has involved even more intensive study of my journals than has been necessary for other periods of my life. Those journals have offered me many surprises. The story I have loosely told myself and others about that period twenty-five years ago is also imperfectly related to the story that my journals tell in real time. And then there is the question of how any of this relates to the Jesus to whom every character in this story, including myself, claimed loyalty.

The events that played themselves out in the Southern Baptist Convention during the 1980s and 1990s were part of broader stories, broader forces. If the events in the SBC represent a central battle in the religious wars, then the frontline of the battle fell smack in the middle of Southern Seminary while I was on the faculty there. In what follows, I want to tell my personal story of religious, political, professional, and (above all) moral challenge as part of a larger story in which these same challenges rocked many American Christians.

The appointment of R. Albert Mohler Jr. as Southern Seminary's new president represented the culmination of a long effort by conservatives to reclaim a seminary that they thought had gone astray. It also saw the beginning of that institution's transformation into the bastion of deeply conservative theology it remains today. As it happens, Mohler was named the new president at Southern on the very day in the spring of 1993 on which I signed my teaching contract.

Signs that the new administration was asserting

itself and ushering in a new era were not long in coming. They arrived with Al Mohler's inauguration. Freedom Hall, the massive arena where the beloved Louisville Cardinals play basketball, was the venue. The two key-note speakers were none other than Billy Graham and Carl F. H. Henry. Graham was America's pastor, known for his worldwide evangelistic efforts; Henry was America's evangelical, known for his intellectual leadership of the U.S. evangelical movement. For both to be willing to endorse Al Mohler by speaking in glowing terms at his inauguration reflected a "shock and awe" strategy of epic proportions. Those who opposed the transition at Southern never stood a chance. If Graham and Henry are for you, who can be against you?

I had been away from Southern for only six years, but the school had changed dramatically in that time. The conservatives had won a decisive victory in forcing out long-serving moderate administrators and faculty. Beginning in 1990, with the appointment of new conservative dean David Dockery to head the School of Theology, most hires at Southern had been self-identified evangelicals, mainly from the north and west, mainly not Southern Baptists. The stated goal of the school at the time was balance—balancing moderates with conservatives. These new faculty members were the conservatives, with more to come.

The kind of prospective faculty members who could thread the needle in a faculty search process led by the old-guard moderate faculty, subject to acceptance by the new conservative administration, with final approval required from the now fundamentalist-controlled trustee board, tended to be people who were not clearly marked as belonging to one or another tribe in the Southern Baptist civil war. It was a very narrow needle to thread.

The student body still numbered nearly three thousand. It had become even more conservative than in my student days, but hundreds of moderate Baptist students were still around as well. Some of them vocally and bitterly opposed the changes at their seminary. An extremely uneasy educational "community" was present, with both the "old Southern" that was passing away and the "new Southern" that was being born represented on campus.

Al Mohler, only thirty-three years old when he was named president, turned out to be a relentless implementer of the conservative agenda for Southern Seminary. He was committed to purging any faculty who strayed from conformity to the seminary's doctrinal statement, elevating faculty voices that would take visible conservative stands on key culture-war issues, and moving the school to a traditionalist position on the top question of the moment—namely, whether the Bible permitted women to be ordained or to serve as pastors in local churches.

Because women's leadership in church was the most pressing source of disagreement, our female faculty leaders were the ones most immediately affected by the new administration's efforts to transform the school. In July 1994, the talented theologian Molly Marshall was forced out of her teaching role. This evoked significant and broad faculty resistance, but to no avail. Molly had been my theology professor at Southern and, knowing something now about the broader theological spectrum,

I found it absurd that she would be considered out of bounds at Southern. I found her to have taught a highly disciplined theology well within the limits of classic Christian orthodoxy. She eventually went on to a highly successful career elsewhere, becoming president of Central Baptist Seminary. But that was later; right then, she was martyred before our eyes.

The truly pivotal crisis erupted during a March 1995 conflict between the president and Diana Garland, then the dean of the seminary's school of social work. It had to do with the hiring of a new faculty member in social work who was perfectly acceptable except for his stance on women's roles. This was the first time a candidate had been vetoed solely for that reason.

As a result of this event, a new policy came down from the administration, one that would change everything at Southern. At an epic, miserable faculty meeting, the president declared that those who believed that women should serve as pastors would no longer be hired, promoted, or tenured at Southern Seminary. While some details of this policy remained to be addressed, the implications were clear enough. A school that had, over the years, worked its way around to a largely egalitarian understanding of gender roles was now, by decree, overnight, a place that required faculty both to believe and to teach that Holy Scripture clearly bars women from the highest office of church leadership. Dissenting tenured faculty members might survive but probably ought to leave, untenured faculty members who held the now-erroneous belief had no future at the school, and no new faculty members would be hired who were egalitarian.

This meant the end for pretty much all female faculty

members. I vividly remember one of my younger female colleagues getting up from the meeting in which the policy was announced, running from the room, and throwing up in the hall. It's not every day that you are professionally executed by public decree. It just might make you physically ill.

As of that moment, the transformation was all over but the shouting. Almost all faculty and staff members who did not agree with this direction or this kind of leadership looked for a way to leave. The exodus continued for several more years. The new administration grew even stronger and continues to lead one of the most rigidly conservative theological seminaries in the world.

That part was relatively easy to tell. Now let me try to reconstruct my own story.

When I was brought to Southern, the new administration wanted to show the world that all was not blood and revolution at the school. Hiring people of orthodox theology, academic pedigree, teaching ability, and scholarly production who could be at least reasonably acceptable to both sides of the ongoing civil war was, at first, highly valuable to their overall project. They weren't exactly sure what they had in me, but they thought it was at least possible that I could be one of those people.

My professional promise began to be fulfilled during those three years. I was indeed receiving strong reviews in the classroom, getting out on the speaking circuit, publishing a well-received first book on Christian rescuers, and doing public ethics writing that was getting attention. In 1994 I wrote a major statement for the Southern Baptist Convention on why the killing of abortion doctors is wrong, and the next year I helped draft its much-discussed resolution on racial reconciliation. Both were so important that the *Christian Century* called each statement one of the top ten religious news events in its respective year. I was repeatedly being called one of the most promising rising ethical voices in the Southern Baptist Convention and, in some cases, in the broader evangelical world. In 1996, *Christianity Today*, for whom I was beginning to write, named me as one of the top religious voices under forty in the United States.

But all of this was occurring against the backdrop of the increasing carnage that was happening outside of my privileged world. Most of that had to do with the issue of women in ministry.

I entered a time of excruciating spiritual and moral testing. I was aware of it then and am even more clear about it now. For most first-year professors, the big challenges are putting syllabi and lecture notes together and then attempting to earn tenure. For me, that routine stuff happened in a pressure-cooker environment that was more about denominational and school politics than anything else. Get a syllabus together? Fine. But it's probably more important to see if you can survive the month with your job and sanity intact.

I did not join the faculty at Southern Seminary believing that the Bible should be read to exclude women from pastoral leadership in the church. I had declared an egalitarian view in my interviews and in classes. It had never changed.

None of my mentors believed that women were biblically banned from being pastors. I was loyal to them. I was also loyal to my female teachers and colleagues at Southern, most notably Molly Marshall. I was aware that to sign off on the new regime's approach to women in ministry would betray them.

My journals reveal that I knew from the very beginning that the women's issue could be a deal breaker for me, and that my integrity would be tested on it. Before I even taught my first class, I wrote this: *Women in pastoral roles. That issue—if I won't change and if Mohler won't accept a difference on it—will sink my future at SBTS.*

And then one week after starting my teaching at Southern, I wrote this: *What is the issue today that needs a clear, biblical, prophetic word, just like racism needed in 1953 or 1963 or 1863? I think that issue is the full equality of women. Help me, Lord, to lie prostrate before you and speak the truth in good conscience, consequences be damned.*

When later that year Molly Marshall was forced out at Southern, I did nothing to stand up for her besides complain to my journal. My conscience gnawed at me, as it should have. Nine months after that, Diana Garland was forced out of her role. This time I was not quiet. After giving the opening prayer at the president's request at the faculty meeting on the day after her firing, I eventually challenged the president's recent decisions regarding Dean Garland. He expressed his frustration with the questions I and others were raising—and went on to proclaim the policy essentially banning anyone who affirmed the leadership of women in church from serving at Southern. It was March 1995.

The subsequent week saw my own frustration with the situation at the school deepen to the extent that I joined in secret conversations designed to force the president from office. One might call it coup plotting. I have never disclosed it before now. A faculty group reached out to the trustee chair pleading for help. We considered an emergency press conference. We looked at calling a no-confidence vote. And I drafted a manifesto describing why Al Mohler had to be removed from office. I was thirty-one years old, with three small children, and no earthly idea what I was doing.

On March 27, at the end of this horrific week at Southern, I was in Philadelphia for a meeting involving my old friend and mentor Ron Sider. I was sitting with Ron and a group of my former colleagues around the Sider dinner table hashing out what was going on at Southern. I was in the heart of my coup plotting and in great distress. They asked if we could pray together.

When it was my turn to pray aloud, I had an experience unlike anything I had ever before experienced, and nothing like it has happened to me since. I can only say that the Holy Spirit of God came upon me. Baptists don't generally say stuff like that.

But that is what happened. I received a kind of vision of what it was like to be, at that moment, Al and Mary Mohler. I began to feel very deeply what it was like for these two very young people to be attempting to live their lives at that moment, amid all the pressure, stress, and hatred that he and they received. I thought of the Mohlers' two young children, who were the age of ours. I thought of their family's loneliness and isolation. And I began to weep, very deeply. I began to be carried away into detailed and heartfelt prayer for them. I was wracked with sobs as I prayed for one whom I had begun to think of as my enemy.

Jesus teaches his followers to pray for their enemies.

I did not sit down at the dinner table that night with some kind of plan to obey Jesus by praying for Al and Mary Mohler. Far from it. But in what was probably the most supernatural experience of my life, I was spiritually compelled to pray for them. And when it was over, it was as if the incipient hatred in my heart had been burned out of it. My soul had been cauterized of hatred for Al Mohler. After that moment it became literally and spiritually impossible for me to hate him. It was a scarily powerful spiritual experience. I'm not sure I wanted that much God working on me and in me. But it was transformative.

In the midst of this professional turmoil, a personal crisis shook our family. On April 14, 1995, for the second time in less than two years, Jeanie suffered a fetal demise—a dead midterm fetus. We never got a medical explanation. Stress is as good a guess as any. These losses hit us extremely hard.

On April 16, 1995, we went to the hospital for the sad recapitulation of the experience of pushing out, grieving, and burying an already dead baby. When Al Mohler and his wife visited us at the hospital that night, we received it as a great kindness. I asked him to join me in the hall. He told me that he had learned from the trustee chair of my participation in the plot against him. Rather than punishing me for what he had discovered, he let me know that my actions were forgivable if I would now abandon them.

At that moment I was simultaneously exhausted, grief-stricken, and grateful. I still had a job. Even more— the man whom I had plotted to bring down was acting in a gracious rather than punitive way. My maneuverings were apparently being treated as a youthful mistake, and all would be forgiven if I backed off. It probably had much to do with the potential he still saw in me and the negative fallout if he fired me. But still, it was gracious, and at that moment I appreciated it deeply.

I think it must have been the supernatural experience around the Sider dinner table, plus our grievous loss, plus Al Mohler's unexpected grace toward me, plus awareness that the trustees were backing him, plus a bit of late prudence that convinced me finally to abandon my efforts against him. It is certainly true that the overwhelmingly powerful experience of prayer at the Sider table became the reason why I have never publicly criticized Al Mohler. It always seemed somehow forbidden by the God who showed up for me in Philadelphia one sad night.

By the summer of 1995, after all this drama, I was a whipped puppy. In a self-pitying mode, I wrote this: *All I ever wanted to be was a good Christian ethicist. A scholar. In this environment, I see that I'm a prize show horse that both sides have wanted in their stable. It is not possible, it turns out, to be in both stables at the same time. This really is an either/or.*

Entering the 1995–1996 school year, I decided to try to make it work at Southern one more time. I had been asked to serve as associate dean of theology back in the fall of 1994. To the surprise and disappointment of many, I did not abandon this new post after the March carnage but instead accepted it. I was now in the very administration that I had sought to bring down.

My journals reveal that in the interests of feeding my family and building a long career at Southern, I toyed with the idea of joining others in finding a way to finesse the women's issue, and I occasionally found elaborate rationalizations for why that might, after all, be the best way forward. I was listening to the siren song of ambition, as powerful people continued to tell me that I could have a bright future at Southern if we all could just resolve the pesky women's issue. Here is an especially ingenious rationalization from October 1995: *I am a person of a certain modesty and flexibility about convictions. . . . I am aware of the many institutional expressions of belief in God, even within Christendom. I am also aware that none is infallible. Grow where you're planted. Make your particular religious community the most human, kind, decent, and Christian it can be. Compromise on peripheral matters may be the price of continuity and service in a particular religious community. 'Twas ever thus.*

Nice try. But I was never fully at peace with this approach.

During that year in the Mohler administration, a friend asked me, "Any blood on your hands yet?" I was of course brought up short. When students began to ask me whether I had sold out, I was most uncomfortable. When my marriage suffered from the acute distress, distraction, and moral pressure I was experiencing, I was aware of it. But still, I vacillated between offering justifications for bending to the regime and chastising myself for compromising.

Just six weeks later, I wrote this: *I realize . . . how much of a hit my integrity—and my joy—have taken under the oppression of this place. I have bent to make it work. But your Word speaks words of simple truth—maintain justice, tell the truth, do what is right. Oppression-dictated intellectual effort hardly maximizes clarity. O Lord, meet me in my soul and abide with me as I walk this shadowy path.*

I remember an especially vivid conversation one week later. It was right after Thanksgiving in 1995. After a long buttering-up about my great skills and promise and how valued I was—blah blah blah—a person who can only be described as the president's top henchman said to me, "Just tell the trustees what they want, one time. You don't even have to believe it. Just say it, one time, and it will all be over."

Just one time, you see. Sell my soul, sell out Molly, sell out my female students, sell out all female ministers who had ever demonstrated the gifts of the pastoral office, sell out the gifted female minister who buried both of my dead babies. I could be dean here someday, maybe even provost. Just bend a little. Is it all that important to be so rigid?

This might be a good time to say that lies are the lingua franca of politics: "I heartily endorse X, the opponent in the primaries whom I've just spent the last six months trashing." Fine. That's politics.

But this was faith, where lies are not supposed to be the lingua franca. This was a question of what God himself commanded about church offices in his inerrant, infallible word. This was a matter of such grave significance that long-serving faculty members were being forced from their jobs over it. We must have men of principle on this faculty, men who believe and teach always and only God's holy truth.

"Just tell the trustees what they want, one time. You don't even have to believe it. Just say it, one time, and it will all be over."

I was appalled. I went home and told Jeanie about this right away, in a conversation we both remember vividly.

Shortly thereafter, David Dockery solved my problem, most unexpectedly. He was named president of Union University in Jackson, Tennessee, on December 8, 1995. He offered me a position, in principle, shortly thereafter; after a few bumps in the process, it became official in early February. It did not include the condition that I take the traditionalist-fundamentalist view on women's roles. I happily accepted. It was a golden parachute out of Southern.

So after bending a bit in the wind, I was spared the ultimate test of conscience. It never got as far as a meeting before the president and the trustees in which my convictions and integrity would be fully tested. But I was aware in that fall of 1995 that it had been a near thing.

I wonder what I would have done if there had been no escape hatch. Would I have told myself that my family's welfare was my primary moral obligation? Would I have found a way to avoid the conclusion that a fundamental issue of integrity was at stake? I saw others all around me compromise. Why not me? Have you ever been there, dear reader?

I *think* I would never ultimately have caved, if for no other reason than that I could not have looked Glen Stassen in the eye ever again, and by extension could never have looked myself in the eye again. Loyalty to mentors can make a huge difference in crisis moments. They help us know who we should aspire to be, and our reflection in their eyes lets us know whether we have achieved it. How I miss those moments with Glen. All I can do now when I face crises of conscience is to imagine what he would say, by remembering what he did say.

Those Southern Seminary years were almost disastrous for me. I was aware by the end that I had nearly derailed on all sides, that it was not laudable to move in six months from Che Guevara revolutionary to Vichy France collaborator, threatening first my family's well-being and then my very integrity.

Twenty-five years later, after reviewing every journal entry from that horrible period of my life, I am now painfully reminded that I was a very young man who was unprepared for the professional, moral, and personal stresses that nearly tore me apart, and who was tempted by the seductions placed in front of my greedy eyes, despite numerous pleas to God in prayer. I did not behave unimpeachably in this cauldron.

But we escaped. When David Dockery was looking to take a team with him to Union University, he wanted me on it. In his eyes, I must have had enough professional promise, enough Christian conviction, and enough personal integrity for him to want me on his team. It was a generous judgment, and for me it saved both employment and integrity.

Few others caught in the Southern Seminary vortex were blessed with such an option. Some were left without jobs. Some stayed and hid their souls away until retirement. The fortunate few left for other employment.

It would be possible to simply thank God for providential care for myself and my family. We were given a way of escape. "Count your many blessings, name them one by one," as the hymn says. Okay, I can, should, and did praise God for that escape.

But in retrospect, this horrific experience took a profound toll on me in some deep place in my spirit. All this fighting, backstabbing, compromising, deception, doctrinal hair-splitting, oppression, and suffering was occurring at a seminary and in the name of God. Almost all of the relevant participants were ordained Southern Baptist ministers. And all of my efforts to retain the purity of my vocation and the integrity of my character were being challenged right there at that holy, religious place, not in Congress or Hollywood or some other secular place.

There is hardly anything as disillusioning as being disillusioned by religious people, especially religious leaders, and being disillusioned by yourself as a faux religious leader, and wondering what any of this has to do with the God who created the universe and the Jesus to whom we all had supposedly pledged our lives.

The spiritual impact of those three years took a major toll on me. I ended up in counseling, found my marriage stressed, felt like I was a distracted and mediocre father, and faced withering questions, mainly from myself, about my own personal integrity. But more than that, the first seeds of doubt were planted about whether there is any shred of contact between Christian institutions like seminaries and the actual God they claim to serve. That is much harder to recover from than anything else.

My family certainly did not want to move. I found a journal entry from our last day in Louisville: *With every move there is trauma. But this trauma is particularly acute. We intended to be here forever. A great calamity cut us short.*

And so we must leave. . . . We planted ourselves deeply here, especially Jeanie. She is being torn from her womanly circle of friends. . . . She said tonight, "I am like a child who is forced to stay at summer camp and can never go home. . . ." And [seven-year-old] Holly said, "Daddy, when someone asks me, where should I tell them I grew up?"

The answer became Jackson, Tennessee.

Chapter 7

FINDING A HOME AND LEAVING IT

UNION UNIVERSITY
(1996–2007)

WHEN DAVID DOCKERY OFFERED ME THE CHANCE TO GO with him to Union University, there was no choice to be made. It was obvious. I couldn't stay at Southern. I knew nothing about Jackson, West Tennessee, or Union University. But we were going there.

Our hearts sank when we first set eyes on Union University that bleak winter of early 1996. The campus, in north Jackson near an interstate exit, consisted of just a few workmanlike brick buildings. Almost all classes were taught in one long building that looked like a high school. The dorms were dreary. After the impressive grandeur of Southern Seminary, Union Seminary, and William & Mary, Union was underwhelming. I wrote this after our very first visit: *Union University is a mediocre-looking place, all brown and brick and flat. The dorms are especially hideous looking. . . . I would not leave Southern for it under normal circumstances. But these are not normal circumstances, are they?*

Only later did I realize, after many rounds on the lecture circuit at the oh-so-many Christian colleges that dot the landscape of small town and rural America, that Union University, at least as I found it in 1996, was a typical small-town Christian college.

It was a little Baptist school that existed to provide Baptist higher education to the gazillions of good Baptists of Jackson, a town truly worthy of being described as the buckle of the Bible Belt. Such little towns and little schools are rarely able to build campuses that are all that pretty. But they are successful in accomplishing what their constituency wants them to do—offer a reasonably priced, reliably conservative college education for Baptist young people who live within three hours of the place. Such schools do not aspire to produce research or create a national profile.

I think it's fair to say that this was the modest vision of the modest school that David Dockery took over in the fall of 1996. There may have been and probably were faculty and trustees of the university who had bigger dreams. But it took a new president to lead the community to bigger things.

David Dockery was the last major mentor in my professional journey. He was the one who hired and advanced me at Southern. He was the first to open a door for me with *Christianity Today* and other early publishing opportunities. He first brokered connections for me with Southern Baptist leaders. He gave me an escape chute to Jackson, which included eventual promotion up the ladder to a full professorship, a named chair, and leadership of an academic center. We eventually parted ways. But my journey is impossible apart from him.

David came from Criswell College in Dallas. He was a self-described biblical inerrantist, one who believes that the Bible is entirely without error. (I always thought that the way he nuanced that claim in his books robbed it of much of what grassroots fundamentalists probably thought it meant, but that was par for the course in Baptist politics at that time.) He was the first conservative administrator brought to Southern Seminary as power shifted there. He was definitely a conservative evangelical and was one of the primary leaders in intellectually articulating the case for defining the new Southern Baptist Convention and its institutions as explicitly evangelical and linked to the broader evangelical world.

These characteristics would make him an enemy, or at least an adversary, to many of the people among whom I now work. But few of these folks would have had much if any chance to get to know the man for whom I worked for fourteen years. I continue to hold him in the highest respect, even though our convictions differ in important ways.

Consider David's achievement at Union University. Over a presidency spanning nearly two decades, he took a nice little Baptist college and infused it with a much bigger vision of what it could be in the landscape of Christian higher education. I remember vividly a catch-phrase that was often employed privately at Union while I was there: "Right now our aspiration is to become the Wheaton College of the South. One day, Wheaton will be described as the Union University of the North." I

don't know if that is something David or one of his lieu-
tenants first said, but it captured the ambition that he
brought to Union, and I heard it numerous times. And
he very nearly achieved it.

I admire leaders with big dreams. I further admire
leaders who somehow infuse an already existing institution with those dreams, doing so in such a seamless
and persuasive way that it seems everyone has shared
those dreams the whole time. I admire even more deeply
leaders who can execute the strategies to achieve those
dreams to the furthest extent that they are achievable.

David cast a vision, built a team, and pursued the
Wheaton-of-the-South dream for two decades. In that
time, the school did move from local Baptist to national
evangelical in its reach. Its programs grew, its faculty
recruitment nationalized, and the impact of its vision
affected the entire Christian college network. Four members of David's team have gone on to become college
presidents elsewhere. Shelves of books have been produced by Union faculty.

Meanwhile, the campus itself was dramatically
expanded, and the look considerably improved. (A horrific tornado in 2008 played its part, wiping out lots of
old, dreary housing stock and forcing the need for new
buildings. Our daughter Holly was caught in that tornado, though she and all other students survived, by
God's grace.) By every numerical indicator, Union University under David Dockery was a roaring success. He
was one of the most effective leaders that I have ever
seen. It was my privilege to play a part in raising the
profile of the school during his presidency.

But it is his character that I recall with greatest

fondness. He was not just a Southern Baptist evangelical; he was a Christian. They are not necessarily the same thing.

I have met a lot of self-identified Christians who along the way appear to have lost meaningful contact with core elements of Christian character: integrity, honesty, self-control, verbal discipline, gentleness, and restraint in their exercise of power. Professional religious people can easily forget how to be simple Christians who try to follow Jesus, read their Bibles faithfully, and submit to the moral demands of the faith. This is especially the case when professional religious people go on crusades, in which the ends are considered so godly that they justify the most ungodly means.

This did not happen to David. He never lied to me or in my presence. He never lost self-control. He always maintained verbal discipline; indeed, I sought to imitate his impressive control of his tongue. He always showed restraint in exercising his power. And even when our relationship grew strained, he held steady. He communicated his concerns but with the same spirit and character as always.

Today we are not in the same ideological-political tribe. But I respect him immensely, and I hope I have communicated that clearly enough so that any criticisms I offer will be properly understood.

Union University under David Dockery attempted the project of evangelical Christian higher education in a very intentional way. Its successes and failures therefore make for a very good case study about a way of doing higher education that attracts the loyalty of millions of Americans but that increasingly feels embattled.

Evangelical Christian higher education at its best attempts to combine academic excellence with conservative Christian convictions. Academic administrators seek to build a faculty and develop a curriculum that can accomplish and integrate both goals. The basic aim of such schools is to produce graduates whose Christian faith and moral values remain strong and traditional even as they have been exposed to all relevant bodies of scholarship in the arts and sciences and have been prepared for meaningful work in the world.

Sometimes this goal is stated even more ambitiously as "integrating faith and learning," which means teaching students to subject all bodies of scholarship to searching analysis, critique, and revision based on serious Christian theological reflection. The most ambitious Christian colleges are also attempting to recruit and retain faculty who have the capacity to produce books and articles that demonstrate such integration and thus position the school as an intellectual leader in evangelical Christian higher education.

These kinds of schools must be distinguished both from purely secular state universities and from private universities with weaker connections to Christian faith. A surprising number of American colleges and universities were founded with explicitly Christian aims. It's only surprising, of course, because those aims have changed over the decades or centuries since the founding, sometimes so profoundly that the average contemporary student has no idea that the college was ever explicitly Christian, or that it claims any Christian connection or commitment even now.

At such schools, one might encounter an occasional

endowed lectureship, or a chaplain's office, or a service emphasis, or a vestigial required religion course, or some inscriptions on old buildings, all of which indicate a heritage of Christian commitment. But otherwise, higher education is undertaken on essentially the same lines as a state university.

Secularization comes naturally in higher education, while resisting secularization requires great effort. Secularization is natural because universities are part of culture and must serve culture, and American culture is gradually secularizing. Universities must hire competent professors, which means mainly people with earned doctorates. Most doctoral-granting institutions are secular. Most professors who produce what is viewed as excellent scholarship, and who often serve as faculty supervisors for doctoral students, are secular. Universities must relate to accrediting agencies, which are secular, and to governments, which are secular—some evangelicals say not just secular, but actively anti-Christian (a perception partly dependent on who is in power). Finally, faith has no grandchildren. It is more likely than not that the religious vision that inspired a school's founders will gradually wither over the generations.

An evangelical Christian university faces an extraordinary challenge. It must create a campus culture, an intellectual life, and a faculty that can accomplish its religious goals while meeting all requirements of the contemporary higher education and governmental establishments. This means conducting college life in a way that simultaneously satisfies students, alumni, donors, churches, pastors, trustees, parents, faculty, accreditors, regulators, employers, and the local community in which the school is situated. The demands of these constituencies are so different that tensions and difficulties are inevitable.

Through most of the time that I was at Union University, I thought that David led the school in such a way that it was maximizing the possibilities and minimizing the problems associated with evangelical Christian higher education. He managed to create an environment in which a serious but reasonably expansive Christian vision was imprinted on the life of the school, an ever stronger faculty was hired in multiple areas, high-quality teaching was emphasized even as a growing focus on faculty research also developed, and excellent students could find both their faith and their intellect sharpened.

I taught at Union for eleven years. There were many good days. Housed in the Christian studies department, I developed a Christian ethics major and minor that at its peak attracted fifteen to twenty students a year. I taught these students in as many as seven classes. It was a little community of clearly shared purpose within the larger Union University that also shared a broad sense of purpose.

It's a very different experience when you teach in a context in which you can assume deeply shared faith and values on the part of faculty and students, over against the average modern university in which under no circumstances can you make such an assumption.

For example, consider the culminating course of my program, which I called "Christian Ethics and the Holocaust." Most of the students in the course were seniors, most had taken several classes with me, and most had become friends with me and with each other by the time the course began.

I taught the course to students who largely shared a Christian vision, and so I could aim at helping them think about the Holocaust's particular lessons for Christians. To this end, I walked them through the history of Christian anti-Judaism and not just Nazi anti-Semitism. I taught them about Christian murderers and bystanders and not just a handful of heroic Christian rescuers. I suggested that the Holocaust reflected centuries of profound Christian moral failure, and then a culminating failure from 1939 to 1945 that had deeply damaged the credibility of Christianity in the world. I could ask them, as I ask myself, "What are you going to do to help redeem the witness of Christianity in a post-Holocaust world?" What moral response will you make? The students often engaged these questions with the most heartfelt passion, along with many tears.

There is a lovely kind of innocent earnestness about evangelical Christian Bible Belt kids at their best. The kind of young people who self-select to be Christian studies majors at a conservative Baptist university are especially devout, passionate, and committed to making a difference for Jesus. To have the opportunity to take that kind of student through a learning process in which the blind spots of sheltered complacency are unveiled, not for the destruction of faith but for the deepening of a life of faithfulness, is a wonderful thing. Many are the students who told me that they were never the same after that Holocaust class, that it was very hard, but that it helped set the course of their life toward works of justice, mercy, and courage in the name of Jesus.

This was only possible because of the overall educational ethos, which on its best days felt like this: *We are all Christians here. We are all struggling to learn how to be the very best Christians we can be. We trust our professors, who are on the same journey and want to help us grow.* If you find it impossible to believe that anybody's college education in twenty-first-century America could look like this, I promise you I am not making this stuff up.

But every rose has its thorns, and this is true of the evangelical Christian university world.

One problem is in faculty recruitment. On the one hand, hungry young professors looking for work in a tough job market can sometimes skate through a university's hiring process offering whatever version of God-talk they think is needed to get the job. Then the school finds that it has a group of faculty who are not into the whole Christian college project, at least not as this school is attempting to pursue it. They generally become quiet, or not so quiet, dissidents.

At Union, though, the far more serious problem was not dissenters to the left but zealots to the right. It turns out that a school like Union attracts a substantial number of seriously hard-right faculty members. That's because candidates will never be disqualified for being too conservative in their faith, and because people who are that conservative in their faith either can't get hired at more secular schools or wouldn't want to try.

But conservative faith comes in a variety of flavors. At Union there were young-earth creationist conservatives, fundamentalist Southern Baptist conservatives, deep-fried Old South conservatives, GOP-operative conservatives, "quiver-full" patriarchal conservatives growing exceedingly large families because they do not believe in birth control, laissez-faire libertarian conservatives, and in largest numbers and sometimes overlapping the others, theological conservatives organizing their mental reality according to the cruel predestinarian and determinist categories of an unreconstructed Calvinism. Add all these folks together, and they change the character of a university.

This is my best chance to say that I believe the resurgence of a doctrinaire Calvinism in contemporary evangelicalism is among the most odious developments of the last generation. I abhor its version of God and most of its version of Christian ethics, and I believe it could only have emerged among relatively privileged, hyper-cognitive, compassion-challenged white men, as it has. But I digress.

As the years went by during my time at Union, the school hired more and more faculty like this, faculty who would otherwise be found only in the most conservative institutions in the entire nation, such as Hillsdale College and Liberty University. This was especially true in the Christian studies area, where my peace and justice, egalitarian but pro-life evangelicalism seemed increasingly out of step over time. Many were the students who came to me in despair after receiving yet another Calvinist indoctrination in class, yet another authoritative declaration as to why women can't be pastors, and yet another snide comment about how everyone knows that Democrats can't be Christians.

I reflected on the sexism part in an October 2006 journal entry: *Lord . . . I am again appalled by the backward sexism of some of my colleagues—thank you for the opportunity to address it. But Lord, again I must ask whether this is the "side of the line" you want me on. Appalling! My sense of alienation from these "brethren" only grows.*

Of course, all of this was exacerbated by a constituency, especially a donor and trustee constituency, that must have been 95 percent conservative Republican, perhaps with a smattering of what used to be called Blue Dog Democrats. One place to see the impact of this constituency was when David introduced a big-ticket lecture series. These were the $50,000-a-pop speakers that a school like Union would never have dreamed of inviting in the past. The annual big-ticket scholarship banquet has featured George H. W. Bush, Margaret Thatcher, John Major, Ben Carson, Mike Huckabee, Condoleezza Rice, Laura Bush, Bob Dole, Rudy Giuliani, and Donald Rumsfeld. There was also a smaller-scale lecture series in which pretty much every conservative-leaning TV pundit was also invited. For a bit of variety, former Soviet leader Mikhail Gorbachev once came our way. The organizers did once stray a bit and invited Tony Blair.

Not one Democrat was invited during all the time I was at Union, even though some of the most visible Democrats in public life at the time were Baptists, such as Jimmy Carter, Al Gore, and Bill Clinton. But they were off the table. Is it truly the case that a university community like Union's could learn nothing from a single Democrat?

Of course, the Christian Right was still in its ascendancy during the whole time I was at Union. The identification of God with the GOP by 1996 was an article of faith, and it only deepened with the election of the self-identified evangelical George W. Bush in 2000. "Everyone knew" that true Christians would vote for Bush and would not consider voting for Al Gore, or later, John Kerry. I had a colleague who sported a Kerry bumper sticker on his car in 2004 and received his due reward—a note under his windshield from a campus police officer chastising him for his immorality. Students who had Democratic leanings often had the same kind of experience, in which fellow students would argue with them and pray for them to repent of the sin of supporting a Democrat.

It was probably inevitable that my privileged life as a friend of the president and as a very visible representative of Union University would not forever shelter me from the effects of scathing criticism when my public activism and writing brought me into serious conflict with the politics of our constituency.

My years at Union crystallized my sense of identity as a bold public ethicist telling ethical truth rather than a careful administrator-politician massaging school constituencies. My ambition to be the latter faded, though I was always at least a little tempted when feelers for such posts came my way. But mainly my sense of calling, and my opportunities, to do public intellectual work grew. I was happy to let David be the administrator if he would let me be the ethicist. This is how I put it soon after arriving in Jackson in the summer of 1996: *My sense of identity as an ethicist in the truth-telling/ prophetic tradition constrains me. . . . I am the kind of person . . . who goes into a situation and is immediately drawn like a magnet to areas of falsity or lack of integrity or falling short of biblical norms. Then I am driven to critique it. . . . At the core of my personhood is this moral vision and a desire to articulate it as clearly as possible.*

My problems in pursuing this calling began in a serious way around 2005. For almost ten years I had made occasional waves as a weekly columnist in the *Jackson Sun*, a little local newspaper that everybody in town seemed to read. My Friday morning column became quite a conversation starter. Everywhere I went, people talked to me about it. I learned to recognize two different kinds of conversation starters. If people generally liked what I wrote, they would say, "Hey, love your column." If people didn't like it, they would say, "Hey, read your column," followed by an awkward pause. Ah, small-town life.

But my visibility wasn't just local. Over my decade in Jackson I developed a national profile. I published several books, including the co-authored *Kingdom Ethics* with my dear mentor Glen Stassen, which became a widely used evangelical textbook in ethics. I became a monthly columnist for *Christianity Today*, evangelicalism's flagship magazine. I spoke all over the country on the Christian college circuit, including at most of the big-name schools and lots of obscure ones in dusty little towns.

In the fall of 2006, David said to me, "You are just as visible as I am in this university." But his next sentence was this: "That's why it's a problem that a gap is opening up between the two of us in our public profiles."

Over time, my various articles and speeches that in one way or another broke with local or evangelical or Southern Baptist orthodoxy had added up to a heap of trouble. The first major offense was my critique of the

Southern Baptist boycott of Disney in 1996, a boycott intended to punish that entertainment giant for extending health benefits to the partners of gay employees. This strained my relationship with the Southern Baptists in a way that never was quite repaired.

During the George W. Bush years, I made waves when I occasionally challenged the evangelical president's policies or questioned his faithfulness to the Christian values he espoused. This was always problematic, given the nature of the Union constituency.

Already in May 2005 I was writing this in my journal: *It's time to move on. . . . I have been trying to relate to these SBC people for twelve years, and it just isn't ever going to work, because they are implacable right-wing ideologues. And I have had enough of being silenced by the pressure of not crossing their narrow boundary lines.*

Still, I stayed. But problems erupted just a bit later when I became involved as a national leader on two hotly contested issues: climate change and torture. I was the main drafter of a statement called the Evangelical Climate Initiative "Call to Action" that was released in February 2006. That statement argued that climate change was real, that its impacts were likely to be significant, that it would have a disproportionate impact on the world's poor, and that every sector of society, including government, business, and religion, must respond. I argued that Christians were obligated to take climate change seriously based on love of God and neighbor.

Sponsored by the Evangelical Environmental Network, the statement came at the high point of U.S. evangelicalism's brief willingness to take climate change seriously. It was a sign-on statement, one of many I have been involved with in my career. The goal was to sign up as many evangelical luminaries as possible, both to gain credibility for the climate change issue and to pressure the Republican Party to act on the problem.

This kind of strategy has been attempted repeatedly by activists who know that the cozy relationship between (white) evangelicals and the GOP, while deeply problematic, does have potentially significant political ramifications if white evangelicals can be brought to see an issue differently than current GOP orthodoxy. Not wanting to lose such an important part of their political constituency, the reasoning goes, Republicans will move on the issue to stay in step with their evangelical base.

Most of the time the strategy has failed. But it was looking promising around 2005–2006. Serious climate change legislation was being considered in the Senate, with some Republican support. It was hoped that just this kind of push from the evangelicals would win the day.

Dozens of influential evangelicals signed on. These were not just the usual suspects among progressive evangelicals, but they included those further to the center and even into the center-right. One of the signers was David Dockery.

But then the criticisms came. This statement, it was said, reflected bad science, bad theology, bad ethics. Moreover, it was a liberal Trojan horse because the effort was funded by the Open Society Foundation (OSF), founded and run by George Soros, liberal financier and bane of conservatives. For David, the news that OSF had funded the *New York Times* ad announcing the statement was enough to make him pull his name off the document. I always have considered the funding source of an ad campaign insufficient reason to sign or not sign a document, but others do not see it that way.

The pushback on the climate issue came to Union itself in the fall of 2006 when one of my erstwhile colleagues invited climate skeptic Calvin Beisner to campus. I was told that I could either debate Beisner directly or allow him to attack our claims without a chance to respond. So I spent considerable time early that fall preparing for what became a three-hour debate on climate change, which took place at the end of October.

I found Beisner to be operating from a truly premodern theological framework that had learned nothing from events in the world in the last five hundred years, together with a nice infusion of laissez-faire economics. He claimed that due to God's promise in Genesis 9 never to destroy the world again by flood, we don't have to worry about global warming; the possibility of coastal flooding is ruled out by the Word of God. This is a ridiculous way to read the Bible or to make an argument about an environmental problem. It was embarrassing to me that my university would host a person who would make an argument like that.

I have much more appreciation today than I did then for the scientific complexities of the climate change issue and for the ebb and flow of debate among serious scientists. But that is not what our students were exposed to that day by my adversary. They were exposed to sophistry and fundamentalism. I had to wonder whether I belonged in a place that would even invite someone like Cal Beisner to a conversation about climate change. I was raised by an MIT-trained scientist and went to Fairfax

County Public Schools and the College of William & Mary. My father analyzed environmental problems for a living. I just could not believe that I was now squaring off with someone making absurd fundamentalist arguments from a woodenly literalistic reading of the Bible. That's the thing about a school that is far more concerned about the drift toward secularism than the alternative danger of a drift toward fundamentalism—the spectrum gradually shifts to the right, and all kinds of absurdities come into play as legitimate possibilities for conversation.

But it was my decision to get involved in the torture debate in 2006 that made my continued service at Union University untenable.

In November 2005, I was asked by David Neff, then chief editor of *Christianity Today*, to write a cover story on the ethics of torture. I had been aware of the growing number of news reports suggesting that the United States was abusing or even torturing prisoners caught in the war on terror, but I had not written anything about it. Neff, whom I still dearly respect and admire, told me that the magazine was receiving requests for some moral guidance on this issue from evangelicals serving in the military. Would I offer a moral analysis of the topic within two weeks, in time to be featured in the February 2006 issue?

I did. I will never forget the day the article came out. On February 1, 2006, the magazine published my analysis under the title "Five Reasons Why Torture Is Always Wrong." Based on the limited information publicly available at the time, I suggested that our government was indeed mistreating detainees in a manner that could be described as torture, and I argued that torture is always wrong from a Christian moral perspective. Torture is wrong because it violates human dignity, entrusts too much power to government, violates the demands of justice, and harms the character of both the torturer and the nation that tortures. I also said that torture violates U.S. and international law and our treaty obligations. I noted that these documents ban torture unequivocally and without exception, and argued that the United States should quit trying to evade its obvious obligations.

The day that article came out, I was in Jackson General Hospital with our beloved daughter Holly, who a few days before had suffered an extremely serious car accident and was still unconscious. (After some months, she recovered fully, thanks be to God.) Holly's accident was widely known in the Union University community. But it did not spare me a long, chastising, highly personal e-mail from one of my Christian studies colleagues, who excoriated me for my article in no uncertain terms. I was appalled, and I expressed my discontent by simply forwarding the e-mail to the department chair, dean, provost, and president. (The colleague later apologized and did not last long at Union.) It was the first of many such attacks I received for my work on torture—attacks on my character, my patriotism, my emotional balance, my argumentation, and my overall competence as a Christian ethicist. It was the first time, but not the last, that I learned what it is like to receive regular hate mail.

In the spring of 2006, on the strength of this article, I was recruited by the National Religious Campaign Against Torture to start an evangelical branch called Evangelicals for Human Rights. A year later, working strategically alongside Richard Cizik, then the public-policy head of the National Association of Evangelicals (NAE), I drafted and Cizik pushed through NAE a major statement called "An Evangelical Declaration against Torture." I was the main drafter, but we built an impressive drafting coalition and list of signatories. Getting it endorsed by the NAE was national news, a huge blow to the Bush administration that helped to morally delegitimize its interrogation policies from within the heart of its natural constituency.

All of this was infuriating to the same kind of people who had disliked my earlier *Christianity Today* article, including many on the Union campus. Different people tried different ways of approaching me, but I was certain that I was right and had no interest in backing down. A colleague in the Christian studies department told me, "This is a new kind of war, in which the old rules of war don't apply." That is always what people say in justifying torture.

If polls of Americans are believed, long after the departure of George W. Bush and Dick Cheney, many still support the torture of prisoners of war by our government, precisely on this basis. As of this writing, the newly elected president also explicitly supports torture. And white evangelicals support torture more than any other single group. U.S.-sponsored torture could be resumed at any time, and many of the kinds of people I once went to church with would be cheering it on. I can't describe the depth of my disillusionment that this should be the case.

I guess our side lost the argument. But I was doing precisely what I had promised Jesus that I would do when

I prayed that prayer in 1978—following him as Lord of my life. And I was doing precisely what every mentor in Christian ethics had taught me to do—standing up for Christian ethical principles in public life and helping the church resist moral compromise with injustice. And I was bringing extraordinary attention to what had once been a little Baptist college in a small town in West Tennessee. I think that the antitorture activism that peaked for me in 2006–2007 is one of the best expressions of my faith and calling in which I ever participated. And I think the analytical work that I did during that period stands up well a decade later.

All that may be so, but by the late spring of 2007 I was creating a problem for my friend David Dockery. We were indeed *friends*. His oldest son had majored in ethics with me and had benefited from it. We had by then been working together for fourteen years. He had picked me, cultivated me, mentored me, opened doors for me. I had become a great success in one sense, and a miserable problem for him in another. I shudder to think about the number of angry calls, e-mails, and visits that he received because of me.

I want to state clearly that never once did David tell me that I could not write what my conscience dictated. Never once did he ask me to retract an article or repudiate something that I had written. Never once was my job threatened.

But I do remember an honest conversation at the end of the spring term in 2007. David noted that he was receiving a lot of complaints about me from the constituency. He acknowledged that the gap that had opened between us was a painful one.

Finally, I asked him, "On balance, moving forward, would my continued service at Union be more of a benefit or a harm to the school?" He paused and pondered a bit. Then he said he would need some time to think about that.

We had reached a parting of the ways. In many subsequent situations in my life, such partings have been acrimonious. The divided political, cultural, and religious climate in our country encourages mutual demonization when we discover unbridgeable differences of conviction. That didn't happen here. It doesn't have to happen most of the time. But it so often does. Everywhere we look we see relationships collapsing in mutual incomprehension and demonization. It is so sad.

About one month after that conversation, Mercer University came calling to offer me the post of Distinguished University Professor of Christian Ethics. David was in Europe and unreachable when I tried to talk it over with him. He was not pleased when he returned and learned that I had accepted the position at Mercer. But I had gotten the answer already as to whether I should stay.

I had been welcomed to Union with a full-dress reception and receiving line in April 1996. I left Union in 2007 by quietly packing my boxes on a summer weekend and disappearing without a good-bye.

Running into trouble with an evangelical Christian college constituency for being too public and too effective in leading conscience-driven moral advocacy campaigns on climate and torture was both deeply revelatory and hugely disappointing. I can only conclude that predominantly white evangelical Christian higher education is about much more (or, perhaps, something quite other) than the integration of faith and learning and the graduating of students of strong faith and values. It is also about creating an educational environment in which loyalty to U.S. Republican presidents and their policies is not challenged seriously in public. Christian college faculty sign doctrinal statements filled with all kinds of theological claims to which they promise adherence. They do not sign political loyalty oaths. But I am not the only one to discover that those political loyalties are often the subtext of white evangelical higher education. You discover that when you violate them in a manner visible enough to attract serious attention.

Our Jackson years had many sweet elements. That little Tennessee town was a good place to raise our three children, and I will always remember the happy moments at ballgames, plays, and school events. My mind frequently drifts back to those times.

Church life was often quite rich. For most of the time we were in Jackson, I served as a volunteer copastor at Northbrook Church, a "seeker" congregation just north of Jackson. I preached and counseled and taught and married and buried there in a richly fulfilling expression of my original pastoral calling. We were together there as a family for many years, and many of our best friendships were made there.

We also had two especially horrific private family sorrows during our Jackson years. Our compassion motivated us to reach out to a troubled student of mine, whom we took into our home for a long period as an act of rescue from both external and inner demons. We may have saved her life, and certainly her sanity, but her presence destabilized our family. And the January 2006 car accident involving Holly seemed at first to threaten her capacity to ever fully recover. By God's grace, we all recovered from both of these traumas.

We were going to live in Jackson forever. In our eleven-year stay, there were job feelers and occasional offers that tempted me, the two most interesting being from Harvard Divinity School and the Kirby Laing Institute for Christian Ethics in Cambridge, England. Often I felt the tension between personal ambition and family well-being. But in the end, I swatted job offers away in favor of stability and permanence in what had become our hometown.

But it was not to be, because I no longer fit at Union University, and both Union and Mercer understood that. And so, in August 2007, we drove off to Atlanta, leaving our Holly behind to finish college as the rest of us started another brand-new life.

On the morning we drove away, I wrote this: *Lord God, I guess there are only so many truly momentous days in a person's life. I would have to say that today is one of them. There are no words [as] we move from the home we have inhabited for eleven years. Today. A home echoing with the sounds of our loving family. We leave Holly. We leave Union. We leave grandparents. All at my decision—in response to your calling, I believe. But still—what a responsibility.*

Chapter 8

GETTING USED TO
A NEW HOME

MERCER UNIVERSITY
(2007–)

YOU ARE NOT REALLY ONE OF US. SO SIGNALED UNION University and its Southern Baptists when I moved to Mercer University. Are you really one of us? So wondered Mercer and its moderate Baptists when I moved from Union.

Perhaps the gulf between one Baptist university in West Tennessee and another Baptist university in middle Georgia does not seem like it would be all that big. After all, Baptists are Baptists, right? Baptists in the South are Baptists in the South, right?

Well, no. And if you have read this far, even if you are not a Baptist in the South, you will already understand most of the reasons why.

From the Southern Baptist perspective, to move from Union to Mercer was to move from the conservative to the moderate (or liberal) side of the Baptist civil war. This was treason. Mercer, founded by Georgia Baptist minister Jesse Mercer in the 1830s, had long been identified as a progressive, liberal, or even renegade Baptist university. In 2005, it was abandoned by the Georgia Baptist Convention (GBC), which once had its offices on Mercer's Atlanta campus, where I mostly work today. The immediate trigger was the university's tolerance of a gay student support group. But tensions between Mercer's progressive Baptist leadership, undergraduate religion faculty, and seminary, over against the resurgent fundamentalism of the GBC, made a break inevitable. Mercer sloughed off the lost budget support from the GBC and became an independent university with a Baptist heritage.

Further inflaming tender Southern Baptist sensibilities was the fact that the Cooperative Baptist Fellowship (CBF) had its offices in the building housing the McAfee School of Theology on Mercer's Atlanta campus. CBF was the name given to the new quasi-denomination formed by the moderate side in 1991 when it lost control of the Southern Baptist Convention. It's hilarious to me how much SBC loyalists hate the CBF. The one group David Dockery asked me not to relate to while I was at Union University was the CBF. The CBF was the official enemy of the SBC, formed explicitly in reaction and opposition to the conservative-fundamentalist takeover of the denomination and its agencies.

The same was essentially true of the McAfee School of Theology. And there the connection to Union was uncomfortably direct. The McAfee School of Theology was founded by moderate Baptists in 1996 and placed on Mercer's Atlanta campus with the strong support of then-president Kirby Godsey, a moderate-liberal Baptist with a doctorate in theology. Its founding dean was premier New Testament scholar Alan Culpepper, once a faculty star at Southern Seminary. Its ethos was shaped by the sensibility of the "old Southern." And its principal donors were James and Carolyn McAfee, Union University graduates originally from West Tennessee who had supported Union strongly enough to have the business school there named after them, but who later chose to endow a theological school at Mercer rather than at Union.

And now Mercer University, and in particular the McAfee School of Theology, was where I was going. Sibling rivalries are the most intense, and this was a sibling rivalry of no small intensity.

But it takes two siblings to be rivals. On the other side of the fence, the Mercer and McAfee side, I was also greeted with some suspicion. After all, why should they welcome me? I had been on the "wrong" side of the denominational fence since 1993, and it was now 2007. All committed moderates had left the SBC and its institutions long before.

I received some pretty intense questioning in my first engagement with the McAfee faculty in the summer of 2007. Who are you? What do you think about women in ministry? Do you understand and share our educational vision? Whose side are you really on?

What I wanted to say in response was something like this: "Do you have any idea how much I neither understand nor have any real control of this journey I find myself on?"

I was based at McAfee and sought to integrate myself into that community as well as I could, and so over time, relationships were established and trust built. But the Baptist civil war, which has so dominated my pilgrimage, took its toll in the early stages of this process.

If I had known all this drama was ahead of me when Randy and I had that conversion talk in the summer of 1978, would I have kicked him out of my old Buick Skylark?

I am now a veteran of fourteen years as a professional on the conservative side and ten years on the moderate side of the Baptist world in the South. This is unique. From that vantage point, I'd like to explain what I see happening on the moderate-to-liberal side of the divide.

If you're not from that world, let me explain why this story might still be of interest to you. As the Southern Baptist battles were a microcosm of the larger religious wars being fought over the last few decades, so the fallout of those battles—what they've meant for congregations, schools, and denominations—can serve as a pretty good guide to the changes that have been happening across the American religious landscape, especially those areas touched by evangelicalism.

First, though, a word about Mercer University, the McAfee School of Theology, and their version of undergraduate and theological education.

Mercer has evolved considerably in the decade that I have served the school. At the beginning of the tenure of Bill Underwood, the gifted president who recruited me, the school made several moves aimed at establishing Mercer as a kind of moderate Baptist counterweight to the forces arrayed on the other side. Underwood spoke of creating a university that was a leader in historic, progressive Baptist education.

But while the school has built on its long tradition of progressive education, the Baptist part of the dream has faded somewhat. Two primary factors have ensured that this is the case. First, Mercer as a university has simply moved past a sharp focus on its Baptist identity; second, the moderate Baptist world has lacked enough dynamism to sustain the original Underwood project. Let me take those issues in turn.

Mercer's undergraduate community, not to mention its extensive professional and graduate programs other than the McAfee School of Theology, simply do not have anything like the evangelical or Baptist university ethos that I described in relation to Union. There are certainly evangelical students, faculty, and staff at Mercer in Macon, yet the overall ethos is better described as post-Baptist while affected by Christian influences. The undergraduate student body is growing in size and in diversity, and it contains many second-generation immigrants with families from all over the world. I certainly cannot assume the kind of Christian background I encountered at Union when I walk into a classroom at Mercer. It's still a great joy teaching these undergraduate students, but the context is very different.

A strong humanitarian and service orientation resonates at Mercer in various disciplines and in extracurricular life, but more explicit Christian and evangelical religion is now confined to the campus ministry groups. Chapel is no longer offered except on special occasions. The campus chaplain, Craig McMahan, now mainly spends his time running a vast and impressive international service and student-learning program called Mercer on Mission. Prayer is a feature at most major ceremonial events, such as installations and graduations.

So Mercer feels neither like Union University nor like a state university. It is somewhere in between.

This could be read as a straightforward narrative of secularization, and from my perch at Union University, I would undoubtedly have read it that way. But Mercer, like many schools that no longer have ties to evangelical Christianity, has disconnected for good reasons. *The more parochial and narrow the version of Christianity in a particular context, the more it produces rebellion.* In other words, fundamentalism always produces an allergic reaction, which expresses itself often in secularism and sometimes in the development of a more creative religious alternative.

While Mercer's independence from its denominational background is a relatively recent development, there is a long history behind it. Mercer faced off against its Baptist sponsors in the 1940s over the teaching of evolution, in the 1960s over its early decision to integrate, and in the 2000s over the gay issue. Meanwhile, Mercer's former president, Kirby Godsey, was attacked for his expression of somewhat liberal theological views in a couple of books. Mercer's DNA includes an iron-clad commitment to academic freedom, which stands against the pressures of doctrinal orthodoxy as currently defined by one or another Baptist group.

I experienced this academic freedom in a striking way in my first year at Mercer. I was beginning some early rethinking of the issue of homosexuality and was about to post an article in the Baptist media. I instinctively sent a draft both to my dean and to the president of the university, asking for their review. Within about an hour, I had received a call on my cell phone from the president. He told me, "You never need to do this. Don't run your articles by me. We honor academic freedom here, absolutely. If you ever write anything that gets somebody mad, I will assume you are doing your job as a Christian ethicist." And that is the way it has been for my entire time at Mercer.

In schools with a doctrinal statement, or with closer ties to a religious sponsor, this commitment to academic freedom can never be stated in such absolute terms. The most that can be said is something like this: "As long as you teach and write within the doctrinal parameters of this institution as currently understood, your academic freedom will be respected and protected." I have already stated, in relation to Union, but also in relation to other predominantly white evangelical Christian colleges and seminaries, that I believe there is a political corollary that goes like this: "As long as you teach and write within the political-ethical parameters held by our most powerful constituents, or as long as your dissenting political-ethical views remain invisible, your academic freedom will be respected and protected."

Obviously, I do not believe that this is an adequate understanding of academic freedom, and it is why I would never again serve at an institution that would restrict my freedom to research, think, write, and teach as my conscience directs. It was hugely interesting to me that Harold Heie, one of the most respected senior leaders of evangelical Christian higher education, wrote in his 2015 book *The Future of American Evangelicalism* that he now believes the explicit and implicit restrictions on academic freedom in most evangelical Christian universities mean that they are not the best places for Christian scholars to pursue their craft. This was quite a stunning admission from someone who spent his entire career at precisely such schools.

There is a real trade-off here. Shared religious vision often seems possible only at the price of constrained academic freedom. Unfettered academic freedom, on the other hand, often seems possible only at the price of a loss of shared religious vision. It's a trade-off between competing goods, rather than purely a tale of protecting theological integrity versus succumbing to secularization. With the perspective of twenty-five years in Baptist higher education, that is much clearer to me now than it was in the past.

Just as the divide I discovered between Union and Mercer reflects that of religious higher education in America generally, so the dynamism—or, frankly, lack thereof—in moderate Baptist life provides a window into post-evangelical Christianity in the United States.

Here is one way to get at it. When the SBC controversy was at its height, the conservatives-fundamentalists used to say that they were trying to save the SBC from becoming yet another declining liberal mainline denomination, like the United Methodist Church, the Presbyterian Church (U.S.A.), or the Episcopal Church. They accused the leaders of SBC institutions, especially the seminaries, of all the sins that they attributed to the mainline denominations. These included a weakened understanding of biblical inspiration and authority, a lack of seriousness and clarity about theology, specific biblical and theological "errors" such as permitting women to serve as pastors, a loss of evangelistic and missionary zeal, and a decline in spiritual vitality. These were all evidenced by sharply dropping membership and attendance, as well as a harder-to-pin-down kind of moral sloppiness and spiritual malaise.

The moderate Baptists at the time rejected all such accusations. They said that they were just as serious about Scripture, theology, evangelism, missions, spirituality, morality, and church growth as ever before. They just disagreed with the conservatives about how the Bible should be interpreted when it came to the role of women—and they certainly disagreed with the ruthless political strategy that the Patterson-Pressler gang out of Texas had used to take control of the denomination, as well as with the tendency toward an un-Baptist emphasis on enforced orthodoxy.

This meant that the first generation of the Cooperative Baptist Fellowship was born with a fear of being accused of heresy and liberalism. After all, those folks lost control of their 45,000-church, 15,000,000-member denomination in large part because a majority of the voting "messengers" who turned out to vote at the crucial annual SBC meetings believed the fundamentalists rather than them. The whole movement was born saying, "It's not true what they say about us. We're just as serious about the Bible as they are; we just read it differently on one issue. We are the true Southern Baptists." Their side lost the argument, and after the dust settled and they had left, something like 90 percent of those who had been Southern Baptists before the fight remained Southern Baptists after it. Today's Cooperative Baptist Fellowship at most relates to two thousand churches containing about a million members.

I have met many, mainly older, CBF-related Baptists in my ten years at Mercer who still reflect or resonate with that original founding vision. They are still quite conservative, very traditional white Southerners who happen to believe that women who sense a call to ministry should be free to pursue it without hindrance. They could easily be described as evangelical Christians, and a few take up that label happily. If the SBC had not closed the doors on the women's issue, these folks probably would still be Southern Baptist. Many of them attend local Baptist congregations that are, in fact, aligned with both the Cooperative Baptist Fellowship and the Southern Baptist Convention, so one could say that they never entirely left the SBC.

However, twenty-five years is a long time, and a lot can happen. The CBF world did create over a dozen new seminaries or religion graduate programs, which have been training CBF loyalists and others for a generation. An entire alternative Baptist universe was created that includes alternative mission efforts, Sunday School literature, media projects, spirituality resources, youth camps, college ministries, and so on. Many of these are offered out of CBF national headquarters, some are state CBF projects, and others are independent.

Over these 25 years, CBF life has produced far fewer leaders and people who could be described as evangelicals or moderate-conservative Baptists, and far more who could be described as something like mainline Protestants. Meanwhile, the original founding moderate-conservatives—often based in Texas, interestingly enough—are aging out. The CBF has become an uneasy coalition of moderates (who, it must again be remembered, were labeled moderate-conservatives back in the day) and real-life liberals. The latter are mainly, though not exclusively, younger, and among the clergy, most are products of the new Baptist seminaries.

I think it is now fair to say that this combination of old-school southern moderate-conservatives and new-school mainline-type liberals makes the current CBF look much more like at least the southern branches of the mainline denominations than at any time before now. It also makes the CBF and its churches prone to some of the same tensions and divisions that are afflicting the older mainline bodies, as they try to hold this level of diversity together in a deeply polarized society.

There is a tragic dimension to all this. The crazy genius of the precontroversy SBC was that the entire spectrum of (white) Southern Baptists all had to relate to each other, and because they shared the denomination, they constrained each other to some extent. Nobody could swing too far right or too far left if they wanted to stay relevant across the denomination.

But once the denomination split, that mutual constraint was mainly gone. But it was gone asymmetrically. The new Southern Baptist Convention could indulge its conservative theological and political wishes almost without constraint. The new SBC doctrinal statement (published in 2000) could write in conservative theological and political positions on abortion, gender, family, Bible, and so on without hindrance, and raise them to the same doctrinal level as the incarnation and resurrection of Christ. But the Cooperative Baptist Fellowship still had to look over its right shoulder, partly because much of its constituency was still very much Southern Baptist and still tied to the SBC, and partly because it was born with an instinctive anxiety about being called liberal.

But twenty-five years later, much of the younger constituency really is liberal on most metrics one could dream up. I am not talking here about political liberalism, or taking progressive stands on social issues based on a serious reading of the Bible. I mean something more like this: They do not talk much about the positive meaning of biblical inspiration and authority, they tend to be underdeveloped theologically, they don't embrace evangelism, their missions efforts tend to be service-oriented more than proclamation-oriented, and so on. Strikingly, many also are attracted to older mainline styles of worship, so that many a moderate Baptist worship service resembles what would go on at the Methodist or Presbyterian church down the road. In relation to them, I am relatively conservative. I might even be viewed as an evangelical. Go figure.

I said earlier that fundamentalism produces secularism unless a creative religious alternative is developed. It is not at all fair to say that the moderate/CBF world has defaulted to secularism, but I do think it is fair to say that there has thus far been little visible sign that a powerful, creative, and dynamic Christian alternative has been developed from within the ex–Southern Baptist world. Lacking that, the most ready-to-hand model has been found in the mainline churches, which—even though they are fading—still offer this community a preferred alternative to what the SBC is doing.

In the fall of 2016, I accepted a call to become interim pastor of my home church, First Baptist Decatur, layering that responsibility on top of my teaching and administrative responsibilities. I said yes in part because this is my home church and it was in trouble, and in part because I thought that maybe it was time to see if I could lead a congregation into creating the kind of dynamic Christian alternative that I have been discussing. I have emphasized passionate shared commitment to Jesus, recovery of profound worship, Bible study, mutual care, economic sharing, and missional service, and strategic innovative outreach to our fast-moving, progressive community in Decatur. As I write, it is too early to judge the effectiveness of this vision, but it does represent my best effort to chart a new way forward.

So this is the world I now inhabit. I came as a scarred outsider and gained a few more scars in the transition. But I am at home here. I serve Mercer University undergraduates in Macon, seminarians at the McAfee School of Theology in Atlanta, and church folk at the First Baptist Church of Decatur. I have given up my restless quest for Someplace Else. I hope to retire here and live in this house, surrounded by my family and friends, for the rest of my life.

Chapter 9

EVERY LIBERAL'S
FAVORITE EVANGELICAL

(2004–2013)

IT MIGHT APPEAR THAT MY STORY HAS REACHED ITS CLOSE. But in the last movement of this memoir, I need to zoom out from the local to the national. My story is not complete if I do not tell you about events that happened far beyond the confines of the universities I was serving at the time. These next two chapters come as a pair. The first describes my rise in the evangelical firmament, and what happened "up there"; the next describes my fall from that very same exalted place.

I am describing this period from roughly 2004 to 2013 as a time when I was every liberal's favorite evangelical. For this claim to make any sense, I must begin by establishing my evangelical bona fides in a bit more detail, and describe what it was like to be a rising star in the evangelical world.

The first thing to remember is that in the U.S. context, we are talking about a religious community, or coalition of communities, that may number as many as one hundred million people. These theologically conservative Baptists, Methodists, Anglicans, Lutherans, Calvinists, Mennonites, Pentecostals, Congregationalists, nondenominationalists, and so on are everywhere, but they are especially strong in the South and the Midwest.

The evangelicals are home to most of the largest and most vital congregations in the country. The most prominent pastors in the country are evangelicals, such as Rick Warren, Bill Hybels, and Andy Stanley. Evangelicals are served by over 120 conservative Christian colleges and are organized under the umbrella of the Council for Christian Colleges and Universities. The biggest and most prominent campus ministries, such as InterVarsity Christian Fellowship, also identify as evangelical. Ministerial students in this community go to one of dozens of conservative evangelical seminaries, some of them denominational and others independent. Besides the big Southern Baptist schools, the largest of these is Fuller Seminary in Pasadena. Publishing in this community is led especially by *Christianity Today* and its affiliated magazines. A robust book industry, centered in the Midwest, features such presses as Baker, InterVarsity, Zondervan, and—somewhat to their left—Eerdmans. The main umbrella group that attempts to organize and speak for this community is the National Association of Evangelicals.

All of these institutions also serve a global evangelical community that may number as many as 600 million souls. Many global evangelicals study and publish with the institutions I just named. There are also innumerable parallel evangelical organizations all over the world, including congregations, Bible colleges, seminaries, magazines, and publishing companies.

Especially in the decade from 2004 to 2013, I was constantly invited to participate in the activities of almost every branch of evangelical life that I have just named.

In one sense, it wasn't difficult to emerge as an intellectual leader in this world. I am not the first to say that "the evangelical mind" has been somewhat underdeveloped. Evangelical historian Mark Noll wrote in 1995 about *The Scandal of the Evangelical Mind*, and he knew what he was talking about—that there isn't much of one. My analysis is that if evangelicals are best identified as essentially a massively successful rebranding effort of old-school fundamentalism, the starting point from which the modern evangelical community emerged was obscurantist and provincial, routinely anti-intellectual, antiscience, and antimodern. It has only been seventy years since evangelicalism emerged from this musty closet, and it sometimes shows.

The fact that my discipline is Christian ethics also proved especially advantageous in gaining a wide hearing in the evangelical world. We live in a time in which moral, notably social-political, issues are of much greater public interest than obscure doctrinal arguments. Nobody outside of our little tribe cares about predestination versus free will, but everyone seems to care about abortion, war, and the death penalty. As a scholar rooted in the evangelical community but fluent in these and other contemporary issues, I had doors flung open to me as a lecturer, writer, and consultant.

And so the whirlwind began. One opportunity led to another: lectures at Fuller, Wheaton, Calvin, Gordon, Baylor, and a hundred other lesser known schools; a regular column and some cover stories for *Christianity Today*; books with InterVarsity, Baker, Broadman & Holman, Baylor, Thomas Nelson, and Eerdmans; invitations to work on various projects and speak to the Council for Christian Colleges and Universities and to the National Association of Evangelicals; guest teaching at Fuller Seminary, where my dear friend Glen Stassen taught after 1996; and teaching and lecturing in evangelical schools in Europe, Latin America, Australia, and Canada. It was flattering, lucrative, and fun, though often exhausting. I assumed this was now just my life and that it would last as long as I wanted.

My work as a center-left evangelical ethicist began to be noticed by people outside of the evangelical world beginning around 2004. I am not here speaking of other scholars or other religious folks but of Washington-based political activists, organizers, and politicians. I am quite sure that this had much to do with my coming to prominence after twenty-five years of Christian Right dominance of the faith and public life conversation in America. Some smart people looking for a counter-weight to the Christian Right, and to its role in helping politicians like George W. Bush get elected and reelected began to see some potential in relating to me and people like me.

This began my brief but fascinating season as what I am calling "every liberal's favorite evangelical." The strategy of mobilizing dissenting, non-right-wing Christian evangelicals for various causes began to seem almost ubiquitous, and when such efforts were made, I was usually in the room.

There was first the climate change work that I mentioned earlier. The idea was to help often antigreen evangelicals come to care about the environment generally and climate change in particular. There had already been smart evangelicals attempting to move their tribe in this direction as far back as the 1980s, with pioneers such as Calvin DeWitt leading the way. But once the push for climate change legislation became serious, heavyweights from the scientific and advocacy world began looking for evangelical partners.

In late November 2005, I participated in a meeting at Melhana Plantation near Thomasville, Georgia. This gathering of about a dozen leading scientists and another dozen leading evangelicals was organized by Eric Chivian of Harvard Medical School and Richard Cizik, then of the National Association of Evangelicals. I got to meet such luminaries as famed Harvard biologist E. O. Wilson, climatologist James Hansen of NASA, and naturalist Carl Safina. We agreed on a joint statement to address climate change (which I drafted) and undertook some advocacy together. It ultimately came to little, but it was an unforgettable experience.

Around 2005, the Washington-based Faith in Public Life (FPL) organization came to me. In an effort led by the very skilled Katie Barge, FPL developed a media strategy to elevate dissenting evangelical voices as counter to the Christian Right, and to get national religion and political reporters to interview us and not just

James Dobson, Tony Perkins, and Pat Robertson. Especially given the disillusionment with George W. Bush that had set in around that time, the effort was timely and quite successful. When I wrote an opinion piece, FPL made sure it got in the right hands, and my media work increased dramatically.

The culmination of this relationship came when Katie managed to pull together a "Compassion Forum" at Messiah College in April 2008. This event, involving Barack Obama and Hillary Clinton (John McCain declined the invitation) and televised on CNN, gave a select group of us the opportunity to ask the candidates a faith-tinged, compassion-related policy question. I got to ask Barack Obama what he was going to do about torture. You can still see me looking really nervous on YouTube, forever asking this question, which Obama nailed. It sure is good to know that the torture issue got settled in American politics that day (sigh).

In 2007–2008, Third Way, the center-left Democratic think tank in Washington, contacted me for a project to find common ground between evangelicals and liberals on a range of issues, including employment nondiscrimination legislation to protect gay people. Under the patient direction of Rachel Laser, we made intellectual progress and built relationships across the evangelical-liberal divide.

I have already mentioned the antitorture campaign that began in 2006. That work had a series of peak moments, including the *Christianity Today* article in 2006, the amazing 39-to-1 NAE board vote for our declaration against torture in 2007, joint work in 2008 with the Center for Victims of Torture and the National

Religious Campaign Against Torture for a declaration of principles on torture that made its way into the new administration's policies, and my service on a 2010–2013 blue-ribbon bipartisan commission on torture sponsored by the Constitution Project.

This has been rewarding work. I have been especially struck by the contrast in moral sensibility between secular human rights activists who believe in a strict ban on torture and supposedly devout evangelical Christians who do not. I know on which side my sympathies lie, which is disorienting, because I used to believe Christians were the good guys.

Also in 2007, a political candidate named Barack Obama reached out to me. In what appeared to be a personal letter, he said, "I am familiar with your tremendous work at Union University. . . . I look forward to talking with you in person at some point in the not too distant future." That personal meeting never happened, but I was wired into the Obama faith outreach effort from that time until the end of his administration in 2017.

I remember one event with special vividness. I was invited to speak on a daytime panel at the 2008 Democratic National Convention in Denver. I took my daughter Marie for an unforgettable two-day daddy-daughter trip. One morning we wandered into an early prayer breakfast led by some of the old lions of the civil rights movement. The Rev. Joseph Lowery was saying to those gathered that although Barack Obama may not be exactly a movement guy, and we may have to march into the Oval Office sometimes and challenge him, he is still our guy, and he deserves our full support. We crossed arms at the end and sang "We Shall Overcome." Marie, then sixteen, wept profusely, just as we both wept when watching TV on election night, as history was made and Barack and Michelle Obama greeted the crowd in Chicago on an unseasonably warm November night. It seems so very long ago now.

Let's face it. I am a registered Democrat. I didn't know how deep-dyed a Democrat I was until leafing through my 1976 junior-high yearbook and seeing that someone had written me a yearbook note lamenting my support for that "peanut farmer" Jimmy Carter. I have voted Democratic in every presidential election since 1980. Sue me. When Randy led me to Christ in 1978, he neglected to tell me that voting Republican would soon become part of evangelical orthodoxy.

So for about a decade I became every liberal's favorite evangelical, in part because my reading of the demands of Jesus aligns me more closely (though never absolutely) with the agenda of today's Democratic Party than any other alternative. This only seems noteworthy in a particular era in which *GOP = (white) evangelical* in the same way that *search = Google* and *lip balm = ChapStick*. The brand merger between the Republican Party and white evangelicals did not have to happen, either in a historical or an ethical sense. The materials of the Christian ethic itself could easily have led to a different politics, as they did for Sojourner Truth and Walter Rauschenbusch and Martin Luther King Jr. and many others.

There were so many cool experiences. One of my favorites happened in June 2008, when my brilliant friend Tyler Wigg-Stevenson, who had founded the anti-nuke Two Futures Project, leveraged his connections to get a group of evangelical leaders together with some senior, long-retired Reagan administration officials who had become, of all things, nuclear abolitionists. We met at Stanford's conservative Hoover Institution. The principals on the Reagan side were former secretary of state George Shultz and former defense secretary William Perry. I had a delightful dinner conversation with Secretary Perry, but while the event was another lovely experience, it did not bear obvious fruit.

In 2010, I participated in a very tense, very high-level conversation at Princeton University on abortion. Organized mainly by a friend, Catholic ethicist Charlie Camosy, it brought together stridently pro-life and stridently pro-choice scholars and activists for an attempt at conversation. My compassionate, "soft" pro-life position was a bridge builder and helped participants find at least some common ground. That event led to a chance for further dialogue, with pro-choice veteran Frances Kissling, on Krista Tippett's *On Being* radio show and then a travel experience with her and others to the Women Deliver conference in Kuala Lumpur, Malaysia. A reasonable evangelical that liberals can talk to—that was my shtick for a while, and it offered many profound moments.

Being a useful Democrat-leaning evangelical had its advantages, both for me and for those who discovered me. My own platform and opportunities grew dramatically, and most everyone who wanted to claim me for their cause attempted to do so. For a long while, the man-bites-dog story line worked. "Top evangelicals fight Bush administration on torture and climate"—that was a juicy bit for reporters looking for a story.

I do know that when politicians and political

operatives reach out to religious leaders and academics, they always have an angle. It is never altruistic, and it is rarely to seek advice. The aim is to win votes, either for a candidate or a piece of legislation. Every panel discussion, every conference call with the White House, every apparently earnest consultation about this or that issue aims to help their side win and the other side lose.

The crassness of the DC political game came home to me at the 2008 Democratic Convention itself. I had been asked to speak at a Faith Caucus panel discussing torture. I said yes, contingent on it not being treated as an endorsement. (I have never publicly endorsed a candidate.)

The first thing I noticed was the long line of Barack Obama banners directly behind the platform where all of us would be speaking, in perfect view of the cameras. Only then did I discover that what I had naively thought was a religious leaders panel discussion was in fact a religious-leaders-who-endorse-Barack-Obama panel discussion.

Then, during the panel, I noticed that the young moderator was typing on his cell phone below the table much of the time and only half-attending to the panel that he was supposedly moderating. While I was duly impressed with this operative's ability to type below the table without looking at the keypad, I did wonder, exactly what was the point of our panel discussion? I know now—the point was that we evangelical leaders were there at all. What was said at the panel didn't matter a bit. It was a photo op.

After a while, the joys of being useful in this way faded. It was fun to be invited to the White House

Christmas party, but it was kind of scary to watch all those strivers angle their bodies to get as close to the president and first lady as possible. It was about proximity to power, or the appearance thereof, about prestige, and eventually—yes—about selfies. I was being mobilized for somebody else's agenda, and the novelty wore off. Eventually it was more important to me to get a good night's sleep than to take another trip to Washington.

After Barack Obama was elected president, being every liberal's favorite evangelical became a bit more complicated. Many white evangelicals never came to terms with President Obama, both because they were white and because they were evangelicals; their partisanship, policy resistance, and racial reaction fused in a newly toxic way. Fellow travelers with the new president were less and less welcome back on the evangelical circuit; meanwhile, we progressive evangelicals gradually seemed less important to the president himself.

In general, as white evangelicals felt themselves to be increasingly on the losing side of the culture wars, they closed ranks. The space that had existed for toleration of an openly evangelical left narrowed quite a bit. And then white evangelicals led the way in electing Donald Trump as president.

What happened to my friend Rich Cizik in 2008 was the first indication I had seen that dallying with being every liberal's favorite evangelical might prove costly. Rich was an anomaly. He was a card-carrying evangelical right out of central casting—tall, handsome, lean, and glib. As public-policy head of the NAE for decades, he was the longest serving staff person of the organization. I had first met him back in 1987 when he brought

Catholic conservative George Weigel to meet with evangelicals at Union Seminary and push for a continued hard line in the Cold War. It was not a good first impression.

Cizik resurfaced in my life again during this period I am discussing. Somehow this distinguished man, who functioned for two decades as essentially the senator from conservative evangelicalism, had the misfortune to evolve politically. He became every liberal's favorite evangelical before I did. Rich started to lead the NAE toward a broader social-political agenda and away from a mere family values line. His enemies would say he was captured and brainwashed by the Washington liberals and became a bit too friendly with the media. I would say that on the issue side he just kept learning, but on the media side he forgot the basic truism that when you are a public figure, media members are not your friends.

By 2004, Rich began to be captivated by the climate change issue and started doing the kind of work I described earlier. This earned him the ire of people such as James Dobson of Focus on the Family, who demanded his firing. Rich backed off just a bit, but the overall work went forward. He was out ahead of his very conservative NAE constituency.

Thus, there were already a bunch of people who wanted Rich Cizik's head on a platter when in late 2008 he wearily gave an interview to Terry Gross on *Fresh Air*. In response to a question, Rich said he could support civil unions for gay people. This was far out ahead of where the NAE was then and is now. He was dismissed shortly thereafter, just before Christmas in 2008.

He was now a martyr for the cause of justice, and

he continued to have some powerful friends looking out for him. A group of us put together a statement in his defense and released it online, and for a while he and I worked together on an initiative called the New Evangelical Partnership for the Common Good.

Rich continues working under that title, but as soon as he answered that question, many employment doors in the evangelical world closed on him. In a very real sense, Rich Cizik's life was turned upside down because of one question in one radio interview. It is a cautionary tale.

Of course, the interview question that did him in had to do with recognition of the relationships of gay people. And that, as I was soon to discover, is the current line in the sand for most evangelicals. Cross it, and prepare to experience the ashy chill of evangelical nuclear winter.

Chapter 10

EVERY EVANGELICAL'S LEAST-FAVORITE LIBERAL

(2014–2015)

IN 2014, THREE MAJOR DEATHS OCCURRED TO PEOPLE IN my life. In March, my father-in-law, Vance Grant, died in Atlanta at the age of eighty-nine. In April, Glen Stassen died in Pasadena at seventy-eight. In August, my beloved mother, Jay Gushee, died in Front Royal, Virginia, at eighty-one.

And in October, another shock hit me hard. It happened because I published a book rethinking "the gay issue" and declaring my new solidarity with LGBT Christians. That book was called *Changing Our Mind*, and it chronicled the process by which my thinking had changed. What I did not know was that changing my mind would also entirely change my relationship with the evangelical world that I have been describing.

I will not rehash the arguments I have made publicly in my book and in speeches I have offered since the book came out. I recently published a third edition of the book in which I review my argument, engage critics, and offer responses. What seems more appropriate to offer here is a behind-the-scenes look at what motivated me to do what I did, what it was like to do it, and what has happened since.

My approach to these issues had been pretty much set for a long time. I was a "compassionate conservative," believing that gay sexual relationships were banned by Scripture, but disturbed by gay bashing and willing to speak out against it. In reviewing my journals, I was reminded of several times—for example, in my years teaching at Southern—in which I expressed deep unhappiness with antigay diatribes from Al Mohler and other Christians. But I was not open to serious reconsideration of the normative questions or the issues of biblical interpretation. I mainly stayed away from the issue.

By the turn of the year 2014, I had reached the point where I was no longer willing to sit on the sidelines of the cultural and religious debate related to LGBT issues. It wasn't like I had been completely silent. I wrote a few articles in 2008 and helped organize a Cooperative Baptist Fellowship sexuality conference in 2012 that addressed some of the issues. It seemed pretty brave at the time.

But my work had not touched the main ethical issue from which all correlated "gay issues" stem—namely, should LGBT orientation, and/or identity, and/or relationships, and/or sexual behavior continue to be viewed as somehow damaged, wrong, and sinful?

An affirmative or even equivocal answer to that question pretty much determines all other answers to the half-dozen conceptually distinct issues that are lumped together under the rubric of "the gay issue." If there is something intrinsically sinful, wrong, or disordered about gay people, their sexuality, and their relationships, their relationships cannot be viewed as having the same moral status as those of straight people, their desire to make marital covenants cannot be blessed by Christians in the same way as that of straight people, their Christian commitments, when they exist, cannot be viewed as unequivocally positive like that of straight people, and their calling and gifts for ministry cannot be recognized or affirmed in the same way as that of straight people.

All kinds of nuances are possible, of course, and traditionalist attitudes toward LGBT people can range dramatically from hateful to largely inclusive but still discriminatory. Much of the last generation of church life in evangelicalism has consisted of steady movement toward less hate and more inclusion, but without any substantial reconsideration of the core issues.

Meanwhile, the secular and religious politics around gay issues were and are explosive. As I entered 2014, I was aware that a whole group of denominations, leaders, ministries, congregations, colleges, and so on were simply trying to keep their heads down and avoid dealing with these issues at all—or they were so busy navigating conflicting political pressures that this was the entirety of their response. This included my own Cooperative Baptist Fellowship.

By 2014, many factors led me to believe that I was called to finally take some leadership on this issue. One was that core sense of calling that has been with me in the stages I have outlined in this memoir—the calling to be a Christian disciple, minister, and ethicist. Blame it on Randy, or Kenny Carter, or Glen Stassen. Or on Jesus.

I was also aware of my unique position in the Christian world. I was both an evangelical ethicist of some reputation and a professor at a university in which my academic freedom would be entirely protected. Those two rarely go together. So I had both the reputation to be taken seriously and the freedom to think this issue through from the ground up without serious negative consequence to myself.

My church situation also played a key role. First Baptist Church Decatur had developed a substantial population of gay people in the years that I had been attending. Many were in my Sunday School class. Our church was facing an imminent decision over whether to ordain a partnered gay man as a deacon. Many CBF-related churches were facing similar decisions, and I felt that in my perch as a columnist for Baptist News Global I could write out my thinking in a way that could help both my congregation and many others.

In retrospect, there was one other factor that affected my decision to plunge ahead with a very public open-ended rethinking process via Baptist press opinion pieces. I now think that the many losses I experienced in 2014, especially my mother dying from cancer in a process that lasted through the summer of 2014, somewhat unhinged me.

Unhinged me? So I went crazy? Well, I had to be somewhat crazy to do what I did. Call it prophetic crazy or just simple crazy, as you wish. It was one of my wisest friends in Christian ethics who first suggested to me that grief may have played a role. She said that grief, like alcohol, can lower inhibitions. In summer 2014, when my eighteen-week series of articles commenced, it had been three months since the death of my father-in-law and two months since the loss of Glen Stassen—and now I was in the shocking process of losing my mother.

Pretty much everyone loves their mother. And pretty much everyone grieves intensely when they lose that dear woman who brought them into the world.

So start there. Add to it the fact that we knew Mom was dying and was not going to take any treatments. And she was over six hundred miles away. And she was in what I considered a hopelessly depressing rehab center. And in her three months of dying she always had one roommate or another, half of them crazy, so that after my six-hundred-mile drives I could almost never be alone with her. And she slowly wound down, like one of those old-school watches that you have to wind until gradually it no longer works. And she was slipping away from me and there was absolutely nothing I could do about it. And I would see her, and my grieving father, for an agonizing day or so, and then I would have to get back in my car and drive the six hundred miles again and think about it all for twelve hours.

Mom was my heartbeat. Dad was head and Mom was heart, especially in my childhood. Her love and compassion were endless. She was always in my corner. She was always for me, for us. When something struck her as funny, she would erupt with that throaty smoker's laugh until everyone around her was in stitches and she was peeing in her pants. She loved me, she loved all of us, she loved the stranger and especially the ones that nobody else loved. And in the end, when my baby sister Katey came out as a lesbian in her thirties, Mom found a way to let motherly love triumph over Catholic doctrine. This was the woman whose life was winding down in Front Royal, Virginia, while I could do nothing but sit with her sometimes and try to talk to her without crying.

And so I began my articles in the Baptist media. My plan was simply to take one aspect of the issue each week and wrestle with it until I was reasonably satisfied, and then do it again the next week. They were just online articles, somewhere between a thousand and two thousand words each. I was entirely free to write what I wanted. I remain grateful to Baptist News Global and to editor Robert Dilday for giving me this platform and this freedom.

It was quite a foolhardy thing to do. I was not on sabbatical and was still having to meet my other obligations all summer and into the fall. I had assembled some resources, but mainly I was thinking out loud and in print on what just happened to be the hottest issue of our time.

The series went on, brick by brick. I talked about the most basic stuff first: what is homosexuality, the suffering of gay people and the history of Christian mistreatment, the failure of reparative therapy, the lack of good and just options for gay Christians in church life. Then I set about rethinking the purported scriptural basis for this ongoing pattern of discrimination, going first through Old Testament passages such as Sodom and Gomorrah and the Leviticus condemnations, then moving to Romans 1, 1 Corinthians 6:9, and other New Testament texts.

By this time it was September. My mother had died on August 29. My grief was boundless. But still I kept writing. I wasn't done, so I kept writing. I wrote with a kind of manic, inspired fury that was what always happens when a creative thunderbolt hits me, combined this time with a new kind of angry grief. I realized I was paying tribute to my mother and that I could not stop short based on fear of consequences.

My little series was attracting an audience far greater than usual, and it extended well beyond the Baptist world. A good number of people were reading along— gay and straight, pastors and laypeople, Baptist and non-Baptist. Where was this going? Was Gushee really going all the way to full and comprehensive inclusion of gay people? I learned later that there were churches engaged in the reconsideration process who waited each Tuesday for my post so that they could study it in their small groups and on Wednesday nights.

I crossed the threshold when I argued that the main biblical/theological issue was whether God's created order could be viewed in a manner that did not require Christians to adopt a solely male/female gender and sexuality paradigm, in light of the genre of the creation stories, the evidence before our eyes in human life, and the fact that Christians have been seriously wrong before in the claims they derive from a theology of creation.

People began hitting the roof. I should have anticipated it. I had faced opposition before, but nothing like this. I continued anyway.

Once I had busted out of the box formerly posed by

the traditional readings of the six big passages, it was as if I had reached a sunlit plain of virgin territory. I spent a few weeks talking about other times when Christians have changed their minds about the proper interpretation of the Bible. I started seeing new significance in passages like the Emmaus Road experience in Luke 24 and Peter's encounter with Cornelius in Acts 10. In both cases, personal encounter radically changed Christians' understanding of God, Scripture, and morality.

By the end, I had moved far beyond cautious rethinking of biblical passages into a full-hearted apology for my long complicity in teaching Christians, both gay and straight, a traditionalist Christianity that I now understood as doing actual, documentable harm to gay people and separating them from their rejectionist families and churches. I had gone much further than I anticipated when I started the series. I had become a full-throated advocate for LGBT Christians and ex-Christians.

About midway through my writing of the series, I had pivotal conversations with David Crumm, of Read the Spirit Books, and Matthew Vines, the winsome young gay evangelical who had recently published *God and the Gay Christian*. These conversations revealed that my series was being read nationally and that progay Christians were interested in having me join the fight they were already engaged in. Crumm invited me to turn my series into an almost-instant book. Vines invited me to be a keynote speaker at his Reformation Project conference in Washington in early November 2014.

All of this then happened in October. All of it was publicized in an article published by the well-known journalist Jonathan Merritt that documented my change of mind. When that article came out, it seemed that everybody remotely connected to my world read it. It went viral all around the world. I was at the mall with Jeanie that day, and my phone, as the kids say, blew up.

I received two primary kinds of responses. From gay Christians and ex-Christians, and from the family members and friends that loved them, I received an amazing number of letters and e-mails telling me their stories, expressing thanks, and sometimes asking for pastoral advice. Having been so often abandoned by their own parents, pastors, and professors, to have someone in my position speak up for them was deeply meaningful.

From conservative evangelicals as a whole, I received rejection. In every way that people communicate right now, people communicated: anonymous letters in the mail with lots of vile photocopied materials, angry e-mails, Facebook posts and direct messages, tweets, critical reviews, invitations to debate, Twitter bomb attacks when I refused to debate. It was sometimes substantive engagement. It was often ad hominem attack.

Within days, I experienced a first: disinvitations from scheduled speaking appearances. Hardin-Simmons University, Campbellsville University, Vose Seminary in Perth, Australia—I can't even remember them all. Again, I should have anticipated this before I wrote my book. That's on me. But still . . .

The beat went on. The disinvitations continued—indeed, a few still continue. In 2015, after completing the monumental task of revising *Kingdom Ethics* with InterVarsity Press, I received a polite call from the editorial director who told me that the press would no longer be able to carry the book—not because of its new content on LGBT issues, but because I was now a problematic author for this prototypical evangelical organization to publish. In a rare example of thinking ahead, I had anticipated that possibility and had already contacted Eerdmans. Somehow the two companies worked out a seamless handoff, so now the book is out with Eerdmans.

The disinvitation that rankled the most came from my own Cooperative Baptist Fellowship. At the time I was writing the series in 2014, I was serving on a contract basis as the theologian-in-residence for CBF. I was primarily offering analyses of moral issues and ethical methods to inform their advocacy efforts. None of my work was related to LGBT issues.

But in October 2014, this relationship also ended. CBF concluded that I had, amazingly enough, fulfilled the terms of my one-year contract after only ten months. Such an efficient guy!

With the characteristic paralysis of the Southern moderate, CBF neither affirmed my theological work nor rejected it on theological grounds. The organization quietly dismissed me from service not because of a principled theological conviction but based on pressure from that part of its constituency that would not abide my continuing in any official CBF role.

The "gay issue" has not gone away for CBF, and more and more voices within that faith community have come around to the conclusions that I have drawn, while others remain resolute in their opposition.

On the positive side, for a year after the publication of *Changing Our Mind*, I went on an unplanned speaking tour. Crisscrossing the country, I spoke to congregations, universities, and denominations that either already agreed with my view or were looking for some help in their internal wrestling. It was an incredible year. What I will most remember about it were the pastoral conversations before and after sessions. There are so many hurting LGBT Christians and ex-Christians. They are everywhere. And they came out to meet me and tell me their stories. I was blown away.

Probably the event that most touched me was when Grace Cathedral in San Francisco asked me to preach at its vesper service on the Thursday after the 2015 Supreme Court decision legalizing gay marriage. The Gay Men's Chorus of San Francisco—led, it turns out, by a rejected former Texas Baptist music minister—provided the music. It was stunning.

It has been a humbling honor to be so often in the presence of gay Christians and ex-Christians driven out of the church in the name of the Bible. To be entrusted with their stories, and sometimes with their hope for a better future for the next generation of gay kids, has been profound. My sense of solidarity with them has only deepened, while my resistance to rejectionist (and bystander) Christianity has only intensified. For the first time in my life, I have come to a personal experience of what it is like to have the full force of (white-straight-male) Christian orthodoxy used against you. It has certainly deepened my sympathy for others who have long had just that experience.

Every so often an issue comes along that requires a choice be made: for or against slavery, for or against women's ordination, for or against racial integration, for or against rescuing Jews during the Holocaust, for or against using government power to force better working conditions, for or against mass deportations of undocumented immigrants, and so on.

At the moment in which the moral pivot points occur, strong arguments can be made on both sides, and strong passions always arise. At least for Christians, these arguments and passions are always buttressed with Bible quotations. Only later does authority, or history, declare who had it right and who did not. Meanwhile, in that instant, morally responsible people have to make their leap and trust God with both the consequences and divine judgment.

So there you have it. In about four months of grief-fueled writing, I managed to make myself every (conservative) evangelical's least-favorite liberal ex-evangelical. I managed to get my name taken off the invitation list of pretty much the entire evangelical world I described in the last chapter. My stance was publicly rejected by the leaders of both Baptist schools that I had once served. Most of my former students and many former colleagues looked on with disapproving incomprehension.

I had left an entire world behind.

If I had it to do over again, I probably would have done two years of research before writing the articles that became the book. I probably would have waited for my grief to settle down. And I would have more realistically anticipated the cost of taking this stand.

But, to use some old-school evangelical vocabulary, that is not how God worked in me at that particularly fateful moment. The book ended up being something unlike what I had ever done before. It became a handbook for regular people struggling at the LGBT/Christianity intersection, as well as for gay people themselves, their families, and their siblings. Unlike most books written by academics, it was comprehensible to people without doctorates. But mainly, it was what God gave me to say at the time.

If I had had two years to bulk up my research, two years to refine my arguments, two years to prepare my rebuttals, I don't think that my basic conclusions, or the reception of my book, would have been much different.

On this issue, it is increasingly clear—you are either fully with LGBT people, or you are not. You are either fully heartbroken over their suffering, or you are not. You either see Jesus as just the kind of Savior who sides with rejected people like this, or you do not. In most cases, pivotal personal experiences involving relationships with LGBT people make a huge difference. But even then, you have to be the kind of person who can integrate such experiences into your reading of the Bible such that your prior view of the entire issue gets transformed. That involves a way of being religious that is foreign to many religious people.

I believe that the story I have told so far in this book is largely a story of privilege. At every step of the journey, I had the various kinds of resources needed to flourish, including money, education, mentors, job opportunities, and a recognized voice. For a long period, I enjoyed the acclaim and privileges that go with being an authority in both religious and academic communities. And, of course, I was (almost) never treated with scorn based on race, color, religion, gender identity, nationality, or sexuality.

So getting slapped around a bit for standing with

gay people was undoubtedly good for me. It was just the smallest taste of what they have experienced their whole lives. It helped me identify with marginalized people in a much more visceral way than I ever had before.

And to everyone who still thinks I was wrong and would like further opportunity to tell me so, I say this: We'll sort it out when we all meet Jesus.

Chapter 11

WHERE DO I GO FROM HERE?

After a great blow, or crisis, after the first shock and then after the nerves have stopped screaming and twitching, you settle down to the new condition of things and feel that all possibility of change has been used up. You adjust yourself, and are sure that the new equilibrium is for eternity. . . . But if anything is certain it is that no story is ever over, for the story which we think is over is only a chapter in a story which will not be over, and it isn't the game that is over, it is just an inning, and that game has a lot more than nine innings. When the game stops it will be called on account of darkness. But it is a long day.

—Robert Penn Warren, *All the King's Men*

I HAVE BEEN A BORN-AGAIN CHRISTIAN FOR FORTY YEARS and have had a visible public career for twenty-five years. In these years I have fought the good fight with fundamentalists, Baptists, and evangelicals, with liberals, moderates, and radicals, with Catholics, mainliners, and secularists, with scholars, clerics, and activists, and with politicians and their minions.

These bruising battles have taken their toll on me. I am fifty-five years old, but that's about eighty in culture-war years. There are twenty-four years of fights in those fifty-five years. I am asking God if I might be released from the responsibility of continuing to fight on these battlefields. I have wondered if my vocation might be able to be expressed in some other ways. I feel torn about this.

The commitment I made when I was sixteen was to follow Jesus Christ as Lord. It was so pristine, so simple. Then I sensed a call to ministry a year later. I was going to be a pastor. In seminary, that call focused on the work of being a professor of Christian ethics.

At twenty-two, I married Jeanie. We have stayed very close and have been blessed with a family that now includes three grown children, a son-in-law, and a grandson.

Together also with my widowed mother-in-law and my sister Katey, this entire brood now lives within ten minutes of each other in Atlanta. What an incredible gift. I am completely crazy about my grandson. Everyone says I am transformed when I am around him.

Increasingly, I feel drawn simply to be a disciple of Jesus, a family man, a pastor, a scholar, and a teacher. Must I also still be a public controversialist?

The changed religious and social context has something to do with this transition that I am contemplating. The embrace of Donald Trump in 2016 by most white evangelicals was just the latest sign either of the bankruptcy of evangelicals or the meaninglessness of the category. To the extent there is a real thing called American evangelicalism, it is deeply damaged by now. I wrote this in my journal not long ago: *It is hard to imagine how any single religious community could so often be so consistently wrong. One would think that they would get an issue right even occasionally and by accident.*

To the extent that the whole (white) evangelicalism thing was just a rebranding of Protestant fundamentalism and never a real thing at all, the rebranding has now failed.

In any case, white evangelicalism and me? We're through.

I am also increasingly disturbed by the dumbing down of the national conversation about the things I have worked on all these years: religion, ethics, and public policy. The same era that saw the rise of a completely unprepared businessman to be the GOP candidate for president has seen the rise of completely unprepared pseudo-intellectuals to be the supposed thinkers of our day.

All you have to do is build a brand, know how to look good, and create an effective social media presence. You may not know all that much about what you are talking about, but you sure do look good on TV.

The skills needed for an era in which anyone can claim expertise based on having a pretty face, creating a viral video, or running an effective Twitter campaign are not often found among the over-fifty-five crowd. I do my best, but so often I find myself baffled by how to get on top of social media, to use it for my causes and not have it eat up my time or my happiness. Perhaps every era's new technologies are best deployed by the young. There are some fine young voices emerging, which gives me hope.

By contrast, the skills required of a grandfather, a pastor, a scholar, and a teacher have not changed all that much in generations.

Having been elected to serve as president of both the Society of Christian Ethics and the American Academy of Religion (thanks, colleagues!) makes me think that now is a good time to return to the time-tested work of the scholarly life: You read, endlessly. You think, slowly.

You teach, thoughtfully. And if you have something important to say, you write, carefully. And everything is tested by peer review. There is a recognized and widely shared understanding of scholarly excellence. How refreshingly old-school. It's positively medieval.

I am also, unexpectedly, a pastor. First Baptist Church Decatur has entrusted its leadership to me, at least for now. I am preaching every week, visiting the hospitalized, conducting funerals, leading the staff, working with the committees, supervising the educational program, and trying to grow the church in unity, maturity, and numbers.

For the first time in my adult life I am the leader of an institution, responsible for its overall functioning and thus responsible for inspiring, managing, and holding together diverse and various constituencies. I am discovering that it is a lot easier being the gadfly. So now, in a richly ironic turn, I get to be the David Dockery figure to the young David Gushee figures who disturb our peace as they take their provocative stands. That somehow seems exactly as it should be.

These days I also find comfort from a return to Catholic practice that Jeanie helped me undertake in 2013. Jeanie joined the Catholic Church in 2006. For a long time, she went with me to Baptist worship and on her own to Catholic Mass. Now we both go to both. It has been meaningful to reconnect to the Catholicism of my youth. It has also been important to be somewhere in church without having to be a leader, let alone *the* leader. It has been good for my soul.

For most of my life I have been building and acquiring. For the rest of my life I want to release and let go.

I want to invest deeply in the next generation of Christians, and Christian leaders, and do what I can to mentor and open doors for them, as was done for me. And I want to look for opportunities to elevate their voices rather than my own.

I am especially committed to a much more global, and a much less white male, group of people that I read, befriend, learn from, and invest in. There are promising younger voices in Christianity and academia, from every kind of background. I am eager to see who they become. Reviewing my own story has reminded me of the privileged place of white men. I would like to break the cycle.

I have seen a lot of men reach retirement age and either flounder because they cannot let go of their work, or flounder because they must let go of their work. In a time in which there seem to be thirty qualified applicants for every teaching post, I want to get out of the way as early as is practical for my family. There is a bottleneck in the academic talent pipeline, and it is genuinely tragic for many fine young scholars. I want to open at least one spot. I want to finish cleanly and well.

I have sought to be a faithful Christian every step of the way. I have undertaken the daily and weekly practices of devotion that I was taught. I have remained a praying man. The sometimes slender thread connecting my soul to the Savior who grabbed me in the summer of 1978 has never been severed, despite everything. Many end badly, close to the journey's end. But our calling is to run the race to the end. I pray that I will do that.

A student who read a draft of this manuscript asked me whether I have a message for the next generation.

Having documented how many illusions I have been stripped of, what, if anything, remains?

I still believe in Jesus. Indeed, I believe in him more than ever. I need him more than ever. Some days the only thing I have left of my Christianity is Jesus. And that's okay.

I still believe in the prophetic religion of Jesus and of those before him and those after him who also shared it—a religion of justice, love, and compassion, a powerful source of good in this broken world.

But I no longer believe that the church, per se, knows or follows that religion. I no longer believe that the church, per se, is generally a source of good in the world. It depends. Sometimes it is quite the opposite. When it is the opposite, the only way to be a true Christian is to oppose the church. Yet I will never leave the church.

That's because I still believe in local communities of Jesus-followers straining every effort to study, hear, and obey him. And I believe in local shepherds humbly serving those communities.

I still believe in the power of the preached Word and received sacrament in a community of hungry believers.

I still believe in the life of the mind and the high achievements of scholarship at its finest.

I still believe in the magic possible in the face-to-face teaching and learning experience.

I still believe in excellent writing and its capacity to break through the hard human mind and heart.

I still believe that the truest human language is tears, and the best test of human beings is how they respond to tears.

I *now* believe what Union Seminary tried to teach me—that the most important voices for me to hear come from the margins and from those who have been silenced.

I take joy in preaching an effective sermon, helping a couple find their way back to each other, facilitating great classroom learning, reading great writing, and crafting fine essays.

I take my deepest joy in sitting around our full dinner table when every member of our four-generation family is there, the fulfillment of a dream that Jeanie and I have shared for over three decades. There are ten of us on a good family dinner night.

Now, I am off to find my grandson. He has so much to teach me. Perhaps I have a few things to teach him, too.

CPSIA information can be obtained
at www.ICGtesting.com
Printed in the USA
FFOW05n1445160817

9 780664 263379